T0209448

DECEPTIONS AND LIES ABOUT GOD

A Christian Response

Thomas Eristhee

WESTBOW
PRESS®
A DIVISION OF THOMAS NELSON
& ZONDERVAN

WestBow Press books may be ordered through booksellers or by contacting:

WestBow Press
A Division of Thomas Nelson & Zondervan
1663 Liberty Drive
Bloomington, IN 47403
www.westbowpress.com
1 (866) 928-1240

ISBN: 978-1-9736-3591-8 (sc)
ISBN: 978-1-9736-3590-1 (e)

Print information available on the last page.

WestBow Press rev. date: 11/13/2018

Contents

Introduction

Because the last days are quickly approaching, the strong current of deception and false teaching is carrying many away to the dark, miserable, ever burning, merciless destination of hell. My effort here is to throw a life line into the sea to capture some so that they might be brought back to shore. They need to be brought back to that solid foundation which cannot be moved which is the Word of God so that they might be saved at the end.

My heart hurts to hear the many who were once in church but are no longer there because they have been trapped in the web of deception. Many of those now preach another gospel, and have turned from believing in the infallibility of scripture. Some of the objections they raise are clearly answered in the Bible. And some others, basic common sense would help.

But there are many who are having difficulties with some scriptures. So I have gone through some of these "so-called errors in the Scriptures" in an effort to help some. We know that the main agent behind opposing what God says is the devil and he will use whoever he can find to accomplish his task. He does not discriminate in these matters. He will even use you if you will allow him to. Satan's objective is to have us disobey God and to ultimately find ourselves in hell, the place that the Lord has prepared for the devil and his cohorts. He is the enemy of our souls and he will try all in his power to get it. But the scripture reminds us that it shall profit us nothing to gain the whole world and lose our soul. Our soul is the most precious commodity on earth. It is worth more than the entire world. So my reason for writing is that some might be strengthened, helped and saved.

We should always look at things in light of what God says and not just what man says no matter who the man is. All things must be measured by the Word of God. It should be our final court of appeal. Not even our religion should have the final say. God's Word should have the final say. We should cleave to it with all our heart and never turn from it. After death we cannot repent or change our lifestyle or our final destination. But even though we might have been in deep error, if we call upon the eternal God to forgive us He will do it. He is merciful to them who call upon Him with all of their heart.

May there be something in this book to bless you. It may be some explanation of some scripture, some quotation or some simple truth. May the Spirit of God be with you now and always.

Chapter 1

Why Does God Kill the Innocent

Why does God kill the innocent? This is one of the more popular questions people leverage at God. Their intent is to state that either God is not so good, not fair or that the Bible is not from God. Some even try to use such an argument to say that there is no God. So this question needs to be addressed.

Firstly we must ask, 'Who are the innocent?' To answer this let's look at the first case study, that being the tenth plague against Egypt in Exodus 12:12, 29-30. Some say that the first-born sons of Egypt were innocent, yet God killed them. We must realize that God gave a lot of warnings before he took the step of killing the first-borns of Egypt. He had asked Pharaoh to let His people go at least nine times before that. He sent plagues to demonstrate His awesome power, but Pharaoh refused to let God's people go. Instead, he increased their bondage. It was only when God killed their first-born of man and cattle that Pharaoh allowed the people to go. It is conceivable that had Pharaoh the heart to let Israel go at the first warning or even at the second, there would have been no death of any of Pharaoh's people. God sends judgment because of disobedience. Now, were the first-born of Egypt innocent bystanders and exempt from judgment? We will come to that later.

God is the giver of life; therefore He has the power to take it whenever He wants. At times He takes the life even when it is the mother's womb. God knows exactly what that life would be like if He would allow it to become a full grown person. If God had taken Adolf Hitler while he was in his mother's womb, or at one year old, we would have said he killed the innocent. But God knew what he would become. He knew us before we were born, and He knows what our end would be. God is the giver of life and He has a right to recall that life whenever He wants. Luke 12:20 (King James Version) says God does exactly that to a man who had no regard for His maker. It reads – 'But God said unto him, *Thou* fool, this night thy soul shall be required of thee: then whose shall those things be, which thou hast provided?'

In the following two texts we see that God reserves the right to extend mercy or judgement to whomever He chooses.

1Samuel 15:3 (KJV) says, "Now go and smite Amalek, and utterly destroy all that they have, and spare them not; but slay both man and woman, infant and suckling, ox and sheep, camel and ass." In Exodus 20:5-6 we read, "Thou shalt not bow down thyself to them, nor serve them: for I the LORD thy God *am* a jealous God, visiting the iniquity of the fathers upon the children unto the third and fourth *generation* of them that hate me; And shewing mercy unto thousands of them that love me, and keep my commandments." Exodus 23:23 further states, "For mine Angel shall go before thee, and bring thee in unto the Amorites, and the Hittites, and the Perizzites, and the Canaanites, the Hivites, and the Jebusites: and I will cut them off."

But the following four passages show that God tempers His judgment with righteousness. He does not dispense death indiscriminately. Deuteronomy 24:16-18 says,

> The fathers shall not be put to death for the children, neither shall the children be put to death for the fathers: every man shall be put to death for his own sin. Thou shalt not pervert the judgment of the stranger, *nor* of the fatherless; nor take a widow's raiment to pledge: But thou shalt remember that thou wast a bondman in Egypt, and the LORD thy God redeemed thee thence: therefore I command thee to do this thing.

Ezekiel 18:19-20 continues:

> Yet say ye, Why? doth not the son bear the iniquity of the father? When the son hath done that which is lawful and right, *and* hath kept all my statutes, and hath done them, he shall surely live. The soul that sinneth, it shall die. The son shall not bear the iniquity of the father, neither shall the father bear the iniquity of the son: the righteousness of the righteous shall be upon him, and the wickedness of the wicked shall be upon him.

In Genesis 18:25 we read, "That be far from thee to do after this manner, to slay the righteous with the wicked: and that the righteous should be as the wicked, that be far from thee: Shall not the Judge of all the earth do right?" 2 Samuel 14:6-7 relates,

> And thy handmaid had two sons, and they two strove together in the field, and *there was* none to part them, but the one smote the other, and slew him. And, behold, the whole family is risen against thine handmaid, and they said, Deliver him that smote his brother, that we may kill him, for the life of his brother whom he slew; and we will destroy the heir also: and so they shall quench my coal which is left, and shall not leave to my husband *neither* name nor remainder upon the earth.

If a duly appointed judge passes a sentence of death on a perpetrator for a commensurate crime according to the law, we do not call it murder. We call it capital punishment. If a citizen on the other hand, takes the law into his own hands, then it is murder.

So, if God who is the author of righteous justice takes a life, then it cannot be murder or barbaric. Secondly, God is the giver and owner of life and He has the right to do whatever He wants with it. Thirdly, God as the omniscient deity always does that which is right, even when we may not understand or we don't agree. We must keep in mind that one or all of these are at play when God executes the sentence of death on a person or people. These are factors to consider as to why God would take the life of Egypt's firstborn.

A second case study is when God destroyed Sodom and Gomorrah. Of course He warned them before to turn from their sins or face the consequences but they refused to heed the warning. In Genesis 18 Abraham intercedes for Sodom bargaining with God to spare it if there were finally only ten righteous people, to which God agreed. But apparently there were not even ten morally acceptable persons. Genesis 19 shows the extent of their perversity as they barbarically assaulted Lot's home seeking to rape the two male guests he had taken in. It looks like it was only Lot and his family that were moral enough and God brought them out before rendering judgment, as Genesis 19 records.

God also warned the people of Noah's days before He sent the flood which destroyed men, women and children, including babies. 2 Peter 2:5 calls Noah 'a preacher of righteousness' which supports this fact. But the scripture says that these people had reached the extreme in evil practices. The Bible says that for those in the days of Noah, all their imagination was only evil continually. All hope was gone. As far as God was concerned, they had gone too far and He had to destroy all of them from the face of the earth. See Genesis 6:11-13 for reference. Some would ask, why destroy the children as well? Aren't they innocent? I would like to suggest that in the absence of adults, the children would still die, more likely of starvation. A quick death is more merciful than that. In addition to this, some of these demonically pagan cultures got to the point where they sexually abused children and sacrificed them on a grand scale. Their quick death was indeed merciful given the fact that children before the age of accountability enter the kingdom of Heaven. In one sense God was saving them in the short and long term. But it takes persons with spiritual understanding to see this. The carnal mind cannot understand the ways of God.

Sodom and Gomorrah exhibited the same problem of gross immorality. Their sin came to the nostrils of God. God didn't send mere men such as Lot or Abraham to warn them. He sent angels. Rather than repent they wanted to sexually abuse the angels. The Bible says both old and young men came to the house of Lot to try to assault the visitors. Genesis 19:4-5 puts it this way, "But before they lay down, the men of the city, *even* the men of Sodom, compassed the house round, both old and young, all the people from every quarter. And they called unto Lot, and said unto him, Where *are* the men which came in to thee this night? bring them out unto us, that we may know them.' The word 'know' here in the original text speaks of sex. Hence the International Standard Version reads – 'They called out to Lot and asked, "Where are the men who came to visit you tonight? Bring them out to us so we can have sex with them!"'

These people had reached the peak of immorality, and they had passed it onto their children. God had to destroy all of them. They had become so evil that they were only good for one thing; destruction. To allow them to live would only cause this abject level of wickedness to increase and probably spread beyond their borders and from generation to generation.

On another occasion, God had asked Israel to destroy the Canaanites and possess their land. These people sacrificed their children to the devil as part of their worship; their innocent children (Psalm 106:37-38). Could you imagine the state that the world would be in today if the life styles of Sodom and Gomorrah and the Canaanites were not stopped? Could you imagine the influence it would have on this world? Maybe we would not have a world as we know it now. Treasury of Scripture Knowledge commentary on Psalm 106:37-38 says. "However unnatural and horrid human sacrifices may appear it is certain that they did not only exist but almost universally prevailed in the heathen world, especially among the Canaanites.[1]

People have tried to condemn God for killing the innocent. But we have many politicians in the Bible, evil men who killed thousands of innocent babies just to maintain their power or positions. There is very little talk about those wicked rulers. Pharaoh, King of Egypt, killed a lot of the baby boys of Israel just because he thought that they would be a threat to his throne. Yet, few are talking about that. Look at King Herod and how he killed thousands of boys from age two and under, just because he heard that one was born who would be king. He killed all that was born around that time in Bethlehem and its coasts. How wicked is the wickedness of man. Neither the children nor their parents did anything that was wrong. Yet those kings killed them for their own selfish reasons, and few persons want to talk about that. But we want to question the sovereignty, goodness and wisdom of God.

Who are the innocent? Are there really people who are innocent in God's eyes? The truth is that we are all sinners. This is what the word of God says in Romans 3:10; "As it is written, there is none righteous, no, not one." Or as Job said, "How then can man be justified with God? Or how can he be clean that is born of a woman?" (Job 25:4) Jesus himself said in Mark 10:18, "Why callest thou me good? *there is* none good but one, *that is,* God." For good measure, I will quote one more scripture; Romans 5:12-14 says,

---

[1] Canne, Browne, Blayney, Scott et al, Introduction by R. A. Torrey, *"Treasury of Scripture Knowledge; 14ᵗʰ Edition"*, (London: Samuel Bagster and Sons Ltd.) 1395.

Wherefore, as by one man sin entered into the world, and death by sin; and so death passed upon all men, for that all have sinned: (For until the law sin was in the world: but sin is not imputed when there is no law. Nevertheless death reigned from Adam to Moses, even over them that had not sinned after the similitude of Adam's transgression, who is the figure of him that was to come.

So according to the word of God, there is no innocent person. We were born sinners, and we all need the forgiveness of God. So the very premise of the question is wrong. God does not kill the innocent, because there is no innocent person really. We are all worthy of death, because we are all guilty of sin before God.

Chapter 2

Deception In The Church

Scripture Twisting

The first and greatest mistake that happened to mankind came through the deception of scripture twisting. Up to this day the misinterpretation and misapplication of scripture is perhaps the greatest tool that the enemy of the church uses to get people to abandon their faith or to derail them from the road that leads to everlasting life.

Satan was the first to use scripture in order to deceive. He said to the woman, "Ye shall not surely die for God doth know that in the day ye eat thereof, then your eyes shall be opened, and ye shall be as gods, knowing good and evil" (Genesis 3:4-5). The Bible states further that the man was not deceived but the woman was. Here is what it says, "And Adam was not deceived, but the woman being deceived was in the transgression" (1Timothy 2:14). In other words the woman really believed that what the serpent was saying was the truth, and this inherently is the nature of deception; a falsehood that appears like the truth. We believe it to be the truth.

As long as you believe something to be true, you can fall for it. Satan was lying about God and Eve fell for it. Today we hear a lot of lies about God and His words, and many persons are accepting these lies because they sound good and appeal to our sinful nature or selfish ambitions.

Satan twisted the scriptures and deceived Eve. Note well that Satan has not parted with his great tool of deception. He tried to use it on Christ when he tempted Him in Matthew chapter 4. Of course he failed. He told Christ that he had the power to give Him all the kingdoms of the earth if only Jesus would worship him. Of course Christ resisted and rebuked him. But many are making covenants with the devil today because he promised them things like, fame, money, et cetera. In the end they are being deceived because all these are at the expense of their souls. And Jesus says, "For what shall it profit a man, if he shall gain the whole world, and lose his own soul?" (Mark 8:36). The primary purpose as to why Satan is trying to deceive people is to get their souls.

A lot of people misinterpret scripture for their own purposes. At times, they want to advance their own interpretation of a Bible text. They are not truly saying what the Bible says, but what they think it should be saying. It may be because of their own false concept of God. For example, some believe that there should not be a hell. Such a proponent is former mega-church pastor in the USA Rob Bell with his book, 'Love Wins: A Book About Heaven, Hell and the Fate of Every Person Who Ever Lived', which caused quite a stir when it came out. It does not matter how much they are shown from the Bible that there is a hell, they will interpret it to mean something else. They have been deceived, whether they know it or not.

This is what the Bible says about deception in the last days: "And for this cause God shall send them strong delusion, that they should believe a lie: That they all might be damned who believed not the truth, but had pleasure in unrighteousness" (2 Thessalonians 2:11-12). This is saying that when we don't want to accept the truth, that there will come a time when we will accept the error that is being taught, and there will be a spirit of delusion, a spirit of falsehood. That time is upon us, and many are accepting the false instead of the truth. If we reject the truth, we will accept error.

Chapter 3

False Leaders

Deception from False Pastors, Teachers, Prophets and Others

Jesus warned many times of this kind of deception and that it will increase in the last days. In Matthew chapter 24 alone, four verses mention the word 'deceive'. "And many false prophets shall rise, and shall deceive many" (Matthew 24:11). He said many false prophets shall arise. Not a few, but many. And they will deceive many. Many will rise and many will be deceived. Not maybe, but will be deceived. The sobering word here is 'many'.

From this chapter we see that some of the most dangerous enemies of the church are false pastors, teachers and prophets and it's because of their positions of influence and trust. Through the seducing spirit that will operate in them, they will have the ability to deceive even those who seem to be pillars in the church. Christ said, "For there shall arise false christs, and false prophets, and shall shew great signs and wonders; insomuch that, if *it were* possible, they shall deceive the very elect" (Matthew 24:24).

They will perform great wonders to try to authenticate their claims. They will be well anointed by the devil. Because of these signs and wonders people will believe them. The word says 'if it were possible they shall deceive the very elect". So we are dealing with a very high level of demonic operation in these false prophets. It is so high that the ordinary people even in church will not be able to discern that these are false. Now if those in church who have a Bible and are supposed to know the word of God are deceived, what about the ordinary man who doesn't believe in Jesus Christ? These people will rejoice believing they are in the truth. And many of them will be in church, but not in the kingdom nor in Christ.

We must make sure that we know the Word of God very well and we have a good relationship with God in prayer. These are the antidotes to such deceptions. We must also watch out for the spirit of deception and the misinterpretation and wrongful application of the word by these false teachers. Like the Apostle Paul says, we must make sure we don't have itching ears; "For the time will come when they will not endure sound doctrine; but after their own lusts shall they heap to themselves teachers, having itching ears; and they shall turn away their ears from the truth, and shall be turned unto fables" (2 Timothy 4:3-4).

It is like what Eve did. She partook of the fruit because she thought she would become like God. She did not care about what God had said. She was concerned about her own interests. Here, the Apostle Paul is saying that these people will hire teachers who will teach them what they want to hear. What sounds good to them is not necessarily what the Word of God says. The Bible says 'after their own lusts.' It is not what God says, but what man wants.

Josh McDowell and Bob Hostetler in their book, 'Beyond Belief to Convictions', said, "For the most part, many church and parachurch youth workers have become group facilitators rather than teachers of scriptural truth."[1] I agree with them fully except to add this; it is not just youth workers but pastors and other leaders in many churches who have adopted this method of telling the people what they want to hear. They tell them what sounds nice, not necessarily what the scripture says. At times the reason for the deception is so that they would not lose members to another church in the area. That church is teaching what sounds good to the ears but is really poisonous to the soul; but many people are attending that church. So the pastor teaches the same thing to his congregation, preaching what will keep the people in church but not necessarily out of hell. The preacher preaches to the crowd at the expense of his soul and that of the crowd. But sadly, he is being a false preacher or prophet and he will lose his soul along with all those he leads astray.

But then again some do it to get earthly glory, recognition, money, and the like. If you keep the crowd you have the masses with you, and most likely the money. But we must be careful with this mindset, because many will end up in hell. Salvation is more important than any other thing we can have in this world and in the world to come. Therefore we must make sure that we are not deceived in any wise.

Truth must be preached by pastors, prophets, teachers and all practitioners of Christian faith. The consequence of deception is too grave. To die in deception is to be eternally lost. What a travesty for pastors to know that had they been true to the scripture they might have saved so many souls.

---

[1]   Josh McDowell and Bob Hostetler, *Beyond Belief to Convictions*, (Wheaton, IL: Tyndale House Publishers, 2002), 11.

Instead they greatly contributed to them being lost forever in an eternal hell.

So men and women of God let us preach and teach biblical truth in season and out of season. Truth remains truth even when the majority does not accept it; even when the prevailing culture rejects it, or when the entire nation does not subscribe to it. None of these changes the truth. Our job must be to preach and practice what is truth. Truth has been rejected before and will be rejected now, but at the end truth never loses. Deception always suffers defeat.

We must be reminded that the deception we are talking about will be deep and wide. The enemy will try to use the best of pastors, teachers and prophets to lead this onslaught of deception. Remember what is called 'anointed' is often well received. These men and women will not be anointed by God's spirit but surely the devil will be with them; hence their words will sound as though they are making sense. If it is nonsense, clear for all to see then it is not really deception. But deception is tricky. So we must pay attention to their motive; who is their message bringing glory to? If it is not glorifying God and exalting the name of Christ then it is of Satan. Furthermore, we must watch the character, practices and lifestyles of those who are teaching. Above all you must know God for yourself; have great fellowship with Him and He will direct your path. Read the Bible daily and do what it says. Love God above all things and He will give you guidance.

How to Identify False Teachers

If one can identify poison it is highly likely that he will not want to take it because he does not want to die. Therefore it is important that we identify false teachers because they are worse than physical poison. They can destroy your very body, soul and spirit in this world and in the one to come. Paul says in Romans 16:18 – "For they that are such serve not our Lord Jesus Christ, but their own belly; and by good words and fair speeches deceive the hearts of the simple."

There are certain marks that make false Christian leaders easily identifiable. There are others you may have to put under a microscope to be able to detect their pharisaical leaven. Let us look at some of the obvious marks.

One such mark is that they don't have Jesus as the only savior. Sometime it is the leader of the group that is the savior of mankind or some past leader who may have been dead for decades. For example, David Koresh claimed that he was the final prophet, leader of the branch Davidians religious cult. According to Murderpedia, the Encyclopedia of Murders, "Koresh believed himself to be a modern-day Cyrus, who had delivered the Jews from Babylon. Koresh is the Hebrew word for "Cyrus". The switch arose from his belief that he was now head of the biblical house of David, from which Judeo-Christian tradition maintains the Messiah will come."[2] So he was claiming that he is the Messiah, he is the Savior. He changed his name to try to fit his claims as the savior of the world. There are numerous leaders of cults who claim to be the Messiah.

On the matter of false christs, Jesus says, "Behold, I have told you before. Wherefore if they shall say unto you, Behold, he is in the desert; go not forth: behold, *he is* in the secret chambers; believe *it* not. For as the lightning cometh out of the east, and shineth even unto the west; so shall also the coming of the Son of man be" (Matthew 24:25-27).

This clearly tells us that no man born in the flesh today,

---

[2] Juan Ignacio Blanco, "Murderpedia: David Koresh." Murderpedia. org. http://www.murderpedia.org/male.K/k/koresh-david.htm

who has crawled like a baby or lives in a particular area, is the Messiah. To put it simply, Christ will not come back born of a woman again. It is done once and for all. So anyone who claims that he is the Christ today is false.

In His next appearance, Christ will appear like the lightening. There will be no time to prepare for Him when He comes. There will be no time to live with Him here, or for Him to marry and have children. Such a person who does so is not Christ. There is only one Savior and that is Jesus Christ, and He has already come in the flesh. The next time He comes is to take His own away and to judge His enemy. 1 Thess.4:15-17 puts it this way;

> For this we say unto you by the word of the Lord, that we which are alive *and* remain unto the coming of the Lord shall not prevent them which are asleep. For the Lord himself shall descend from heaven with a shout, with the voice of the archangel, and with the trump of God: and the dead in Christ shall rise first: Then we which are alive *and* remain shall be caught up together with them in the clouds, to meet the Lord in the air: and so shall we ever be with the Lord.

Additionally, one must check the character of the leaders and followers as well as their teaching as it relates to morality. The followers of Christ must live a holy life and promote holy living among other followers. They must seek to live like He lived on earth and be obedient to His written word. Over and over again the Bible teaches that God's people must live a holy life. When people claim to be teaching the ways of God and are living in immorality, it is a sign that they are not connected to the God they claim to preach. The true followers of God don't just speak in a particular way but they must live in accordance to the Word of God, morally.

Another mark of false teachers is their claim that the Bible is not the final authority as we have seen earlier. They always have another book or books that are on par with the Bible or even greater than the Bible; sometimes they add books to the Bible. Again, the examples are endless. To the Muslim the Koran supersedes the Bible. It is their final authority. Then the Roman Catholics added the Apocrypha to the Bible as being the word of God, and they use it for faith and practice. The Jehovah's Witnesses have removed verses from the Bible with no explanation. For instance they have removed Mark 7:16 from their New World Translation of the Holy Scriptures. Mark 7:17 is there, but for verse 16 they have only put in 16– without any explanation.

Many cult leaders say that they have received exclusive revelations from God and these 'deep' things are not even found in the Bible. One such example is Sun Myung Moon, founder of the Unification Church. According to Mr. Moon, "We are the only people who truly understand the heart of Jesus, the anguish of Jesus, and the hope of Jesus."[3] What of the Mormon's? "The Mormon Church teaches that Christianity was in apostasy for some 18 centuries until God revealed new "truth" to Joseph Smith, Jr., restoring the true gospel that had been lost. Today the Mormon church has its living prophets who receive divine revelation from God, continually bringing new "truth" to the world."[4]

Let me explain a bit what the above statement says.

---

[3] Josh McDowell and Don Stewart, *Handbook of Today's Religions*, (Nashville: Thomas Nelson Publishers), 20

[4] McDowell and Stewart, *Handbook of Today's Religions*, 20

The Mormon Church has a living prophet who tells the congregation exactly how they should function as a church. That prophet is supposed to be inspired, just as Apostles Paul and Peter were by Jesus Christ. According to the church, he receives revelations from God. Whatsoever he says is the truth, and when that prophet dies, the one who succeeds as leader of the organization, becomes the living prophet, inspired by God to continue God's work. These prophets are said to receive direct revelation from God. On any matter, they are the final authority. What a sad indictment on the ignorance of people in regards to Bible and theology to fall for these false doctrines.

Another common characteristic found in many cults, is their false teaching about Jesus Christ. Some will deny Him totally. Some will say He came but He was not the only way to God. Yet others will say that He died; that He was a good man and a prophet, but he was not God. Therefore, their central preaching and teaching is not about Jesus. If one is not teaching about and lifting up Jesus, then he is preaching another gospel; and that other gospel is false. As long as Jesus is not the center and the only Saviour and Lord, then it is false. It may provide many beautiful things, but it cannot provide salvation if Jesus is not Lord.

Many of these cults have very strong leadership, and many of them are very charismatic and brilliant. Now this quality in itself is not bad. But when it is being used to control and mislead people then we have a serious problem. A lot of cult leaders manipulate their followers. They tell them where they can and cannot go; and if they are permitted to go, they tell them what time to go and when to return. Some of them tell their followers who they should or should not marry. At times, couples are even told how often they should sleep with their wives or husbands. Still there are others who ask persons to divorce their spouses and then marry them off to someone else of their choice. Some of those manipulative leaders have sexual relations with whosoever they want from the congregation, and it is not sin to them. But it would be sin if someone else does it. With these strong leaders, the followers become totally dependent on them for direction for faith and life. One would remember Jim Jones for example. He told his followers to drink what was a poisoned substance and they did, and died with him.

There are some other characteristics of cults that are not as obvious as those already mentioned. We have to scrutinize these closely.

Sadly some cult leaders come out of good Christian churches and had good intentions. Some came out of these churches because they thought some things were not being done correctly, and it was hard for them to stay under such circumstances. That in itself is not bad. But some of these leaders after a while started misleading their own followers. They fall into sins and then try to justify their transgressions. Many of these groups have nobody over them to whom they will submit or be accountable to. Therefore no one can correct them.

Then you have some who are genuinely deceived by evil spirits. Now, these people may have been hearing from God before, but somehow they depend heavily on hearing a voice, having a dream or getting into a trance; they begin to focus on these things more than on the Word of God and fellowship with Him in holy living. They begin to listen to these voices, dreams and prophecies more than the Word of God and many of them fall away into heresy and cultic practices.

There are others who feel that they are holier than most and so they must separate themselves from the main congregation. They select those who they feel are as righteous as they are to pray and have Bible study with. The others are too carnal or unholy for them. They seem oblivious to the fact that they are violating a biblical principle by separating themselves from the brethren. According to Hebrews 10:25, "Not forsaking the assembling of ourselves together, as the manner of some *is;* but exhorting *one another:* and so much the more, as ye see the day approaching". In Matthew 13:30 Jesus also said, "Let both grow together until the harvest: and in the time of harvest I will say to the reapers, Gather ye together first the tares, and bind them in bundles to burn them: but gather the wheat into my barn."

Now I only mentioned this principle of not isolating ourselves from the body. We are light and we can stay in the body, let our light shine and as a result save some from eternal damnation. Light is no good if it only shines among other lights and not in the darkness. It is always dangerous when a sheep leaves the flock in this world of wolves. We are not the only ones who have and know the truth. We must be very careful of spiritual pride. The devil always enters where there is pride, because pride comes from him.

Another faction belongs to those who criticize all other churches. They believe that only their organization preaches the truth and interprets the Bible correctly. It is as if they are saying, 'If you are not in our church and organization then you cannot be saved, for all others are wrong.' At times, these cultic groups are in less than a handful of nations, but they believe that they alone are saved. If that is so then we can agree that the numbers that will be saved are few.

But God has a great company of saints from all tongues and nations. There are places that my organization or yours may never reach, but God has people there and He uses faithful men and women of all stripes to reach them.

We must be careful of the cult of the modern Pharisees

Chapter 4

Deception About Suicide

Suicide is defined by the Merriam-webster dictionary as 'the act or an instance of taking one's own life voluntarily and intentionally.'[1] It is when a person deliberately kills him or herself.

Approximately 30,000 Americans commit suicide annually, although many suicidologists believe that figure underestimates the actual number of suicides, because suicides are misreported as accidents. Suicide is the eighth leading cause of death among American adults; it is the third leading cause of death among adolescents and young adults aged 15 to 24. For every completed suicide there are between eight and twenty attempts. At least

---

[1] www.merriam-webster.com/dictionary/suicide

> five million Americans have attempted to kill
> themselves.[2]

This shows that there is a major problem with suicide. Although this quotation is about America, it may be worse among many nations which have more economic challenges and poor human rights. But it affects everybody. Both rich and poor commit suicide; black and white, male and female commit suicide. In addition in our postmodern world, euthanasia, legally assisted suicide and cybersuicide are rapidly increasing. Hence it is necessary to address this problem. What does God have to say about this? Is it moral or is it wrong?

There are many situations in one's life that can drive him to suicidal thoughts. These may be situations that bring great shame or embarrassment. Some people commit some grave acts, immoral or illegal and think that they will never be discovered. When the crime becomes public, they feel they have no option but to kill themselves before they are arrested. There are people who, because of pressure at home from parents or spouse, feel that the best thing to do to get rid of the pressure is to get rid of themselves.

There are others who turn to suicide because of economical or financial pressure. At some point in their lives they may have been well-to-do in their communities, freely buying and eating whatever they wanted. But, they might have lost their jobs or business and as a result became unable to take care of themselves or their families. The banks may have called to repossess their property. And suicide seemed the only way out.

At times because of material things or problems in

---

[2] David G. Benner and Peter C. Hill, *Baker Encyclopedia of Psychology and Counseling* (Grand Rapids, MI: Baker Books, 1999), 1183

relationships, people think that the way to solve it is by taking their lives. Sadly there are those who take the lives of their partners and then take their own lives in a murder-suicide combination.

Death in a family can cause some to commit suicide as well. They may feel that is the only way to cope with the grief. To some of them, taking their own lives would cause them to meet their departed loved ones, because they just cannot go on without them.

Some people take their lives because they suffer from a particular illness and they believe that someone of their caliber should not have that problem. Or sometimes it is because of the pain that the sickness brings on them or their families. They may think that they are a burden to the family and therefore they'd rather die, supposedly granting relief to the family and community.

There are times individuals commit suicide because they feel that they cannot meet the expectations that people have of them. They hear things like, 'you should be like this person or that person, but all you have is a menial job.' There are people among us who cannot handle that kind of pressure.

There are people who seem to have been pushed by evil spirits to commit suicide. As a pastor, from time to time I have been called to counsel people who have attempted to commit suicide. Some say to me, 'Pastor, I went to a witchcraft worker and from that time I have been hearing a voice telling me to kill myself in order for me to have true peace.' There are times I am asked to come to the hospital at the request of someone who may have drunk a deadly poison. Sometimes they tell me that it was a force stronger than them that drove them to drink the poison.

Then again there are people who will commit suicide

because they cannot handle loneliness, and they believe that no one cares about them. They see themselves as alone or helpless or having to beg for everything. Some feel that life is not worth living because they are of no good to humanity and have nothing to contribute.

Additionally there are people who commit suicide because they are mentally ill. Some just cannot help themselves due to chemical or hormonal imbalances. They don't have the ability to make informed decisions. They may feel that going on top of a six story building and jumping off would not cause them any harm. Or, by throwing themselves in front of a moving train they can stop the train. This is an example of someone with a mental problem who needs special attention. With them I greatly sympathize.

The person who is about to commit suicide feels that this is how he or she can resolve a particular situation. Obviously it is the wrong way but that is their way of solving their problem. As far as they are concerned, if they take this step everything would be over after that.

Let us look at some references on symptoms of suicide. If we can identify a thing then we may be able to help in the solution. Howard Stone writes, "Suicide can result from several different emotional states, among them depression, psychosis and agitation." He continues, "Other categories of individuals at risk for suicide are the recently bereaved or divorced, gay males, individuals who have attempted suicide before, alcoholics and other substance abusers, people recently diagnosed with a terminal illness and sexual deviants. Each of these groups has a relatively high suicide rate."[3]

According to H. Norman Wright, "Many people commit

---

[3] Howard W. Stone, *Creative Pastoral Counseling Series: Crisis Counseling*, (Minneapolis, MN: Fortress Press, 2009), 60.

suicide for revenge. Some teenagers feel overwhelmed by hurt or rejection from another person. Their desire to hurt back is stronger than the desire to live." Another reason he gave was hopelessness. He said, "Twenty-five percent of those who commit suicide do so after giving it quiet consideration and weighing the pros and cons of living and dying. They decide that death is the best option."[4]

So as Christians and a community we have a job to do to be of some assistance to these groups of people. We must try to comfort those who are depressed. Sometimes our actions or non-actions have a part to play in them to be depressed. We should provide counsel and other assistance to people who deal with substance abuse and the alcoholics and the other groups mentioned; we must advise them of the dangers involved. Also, we must be more concerned as a society for those who have lost loved ones and those who are terminally ill.

Many people think that when they die there is no more pain. This is one of the reasons that this book includes a chapter on death and what happens after death. My hope is that people will seek to die with assurance of a better life.

The greatest gift we have is the gift of life. It was not given to us by man, but by God. We must not allow people to pressure us to the point where we want to take our lives. When we leave this earth we are going to another world, either in heaven or hell. The world we go to will depend on how we lived on earth.

The Bible mentions six specific people who committed suicide: Abimelech (Judges 9:54), Saul (1 Samuel 31:4), Saul's armor-bearer (1 Samuel 31:4–6), Ahithophel (2

---

[4] H. Norman Wright, *The Complete Guide to Crisis and Trauma Counseling; What to do and say When it Matters Most*, (Ventura, CA: Regal/From Gospel Light, 2011), 301-302

Samuel 17:23), Zimri (1 Kings 16:18), and Judas (Matthew 27:5). Five of these men were noted for their wickedness (the exception is Saul's armor-bearer—nothing is said of his character). Some consider Samson's death an example of suicide, because he knew his actions would lead to his death (Judges 16:26–31), but it is clear that Samson's goal was to kill Philistines, not himself. The Bible shows suicide to be as equal to murder, which is what it is—self-murder. And we know that no murderer has a place in the kingdom of God. God is the only one who is to decide when and how a person should die. The psalmist represents this by saying, "My times are in your hands" (Psalm 31:15).

Let us not end this life in suicide. That is not a good way to end. And it may very well disqualify us from entering heaven and cause us to lift our eyes in hell. There is no place as wicked, frustrating, evil and painful as hell. Let us not allow anything to cause us to go there.

There are some religions that will not even perform a funeral for a suicide victim. "…According to Josephus, normal Jewish practice of his time included the shameful burial of suicides after dusk."[5]

For the religious the greater question about suicide is where does one end up. I have had the opportunity to pray with people who committed suicide, and while on their death beds, led them to Christ. I want to believe if they were genuine, that Christ heard them and forgave them. And I believe that there are many like that. As a matter of fact I prayed for one such individual who had ingested a poisonous substance and he had little hope for life. He repented in the hospital bed and God healed him. He is alive today, glory to God.

---

[5] F. L. Cross and E. A. Livingstone, *The Oxford Dictionary of the Christian Church*, (Oxford: Oxford University Press, 2009), 1567

But the majority of people who attempt suicide don't have a chance to repent. Many just take a gun or rope and kill themselves. Most of them don't think about God. So they die in sin and end up in a place that is worse than any place human beings can imagine. Shockingly for them the pain, shame, regret, the suffering do not stop when they take their lives. It is only the beginning of endless trouble. To make it worse is the fact that you cannot die again even if you want to, but you cannot repent either, even if you want to. The suffering never abates. That's the nature of hell. So suicide should never be considered as an option.

There is help. There is someone near, that no matter who has rejected, offended, abused, disappointed or betrayed your trust, if you turn to Him with all your heart, He will give you a fresh start and help in your distress. And that person is Jesus Christ. He is the peace giver, comforter, counselor and Savior of the world.

Let's revisit the final moments of King Saul's life. We read about his suicide after being wounded in battle with the Philistines. "Then said Saul unto his armourbearer, Draw thy sword, and thrust me through therewith; lest these uncircumcised come and thrust me through, and abuse me. But his armourbearer would not; for he was sore afraid. Therefore Saul took a sword, and fell upon it" (1 Samuel 31:4). Here, this king killed himself because he was afraid that the enemy would take him and abuse him before killing him. He thought of what the enemy might have done to him. He thought of the worst case scenario. He never thought that maybe he could escape or maybe he could recover from the wound, or maybe the enemy would not see him or maybe he can appeal to God and God would save him.. No, he thought of the worse that could happen to him and so he took his own life.

We must try our best to defer to hope when faced with trouble in this life. We must believe that things can change for the better for us. We must believe in miracles. As the Bible says, "Turn you to the strong hold, ye prisoners of hope: even to day do I declare *that* I will render double unto thee" (Zechariah 9:12). We must be prisoners of hope. If there is a will, there is a way. Hope is a currency given for this life, while we are alive on earth. As the scripture says, "For to him that is joined to all the living there is hope: for a living dog is better than a dead lion" (Ecclesiastes 9:4). Life is what we have, so let us make the best of it. There are people in worse situations than we are and they have not taken their lives. When pressure comes to try us we must not allow it to cause us to take our lives. The only person that wins in suicide is the devil.

I find this statement about Saul's suicide quite sobering. "To such an extremity was he now reduced that, he was desirous to die by the hand of his own servant, rather than by the hand of the Philistines, lest they should abuse him as they had abused Samson. Miserable man, he finds himself dying, and all his care is to keep his body out of the hands of the Philistines, instead of being solicitous to resign his soul into the hands of God who gave it."[6]

There is nothing as important as a man's soul and we must make sure in life and in death that it is in the hand of God. There is no assurance that it is in the hand of God when you extinguish it yourself.

One of the most notorious suicides we know about is that of Judas Iscariot, who betrayed his leader the Messiah and then killed himself. We have the record of that in Matthew 27:3-5. It reads,

---

[6] Matthew Henry, *An Exposition of the Old and New Testament*, (London: Thoms Printer, 1839), 444

Then Judas, which had betrayed him, when he saw that he was condemned, repented himself, and brought again the thirty pieces of silver to the chief priests and elders, Saying, I have sinned in that I have betrayed the innocent blood. And they said, What *is that* to us? see thou *to that*. And he cast down the pieces of silver in the temple, and departed, and went and hanged himself."

This being the most known betrayal and suicide in the Bible and most likely the world, we must give some attention to it. Maybe we can learn much from it because great coverage is given to it in other verses of the Bible.

It is highly possible that Judas was suffering with a terrible character defect of the love of money. Money controlled him. He would do anything for money, even betray his own master. But I am also of the view that Judas thought that Christ would have escaped from the hands of His enemy. Therefore he, Judas, felt free to receive the money. He would have been paid for a job, and yet Christ would have escaped. So he would not be at fault since Christ would not be arrested or killed. But things didn't go Judas' way. Christ did not seek to escape. Instead they did arrest Him and He never fought back. When Judas saw that, he went to return the money to the High Priest, but it was not received at his hand. Then the weight of his crime fell on him. So he went and hanged himself, seeing he had betrayed innocent blood.

Judas' betrayal of Jesus was prompted by the devil. We read from scripture, "Then entered Satan into Judas surnamed Iscariot, being of the number of the twelve. And he went his way, and communed with the chief priests and captains, how he might betray him unto them. And they were glad, and covenanted to give him money" (Luke 22:3-5). I believe that the same devil which entered Judas never left him until he had influenced him to take his own life. The devil brought all manner of reasons to his head to justify why he should take his own life, including guilt and shame. He may have said to Judas, 'You betrayed an innocent man, your own leader, the Saviour.' The devil probably taunted him by asking, 'What can you do with this money? What will your friends and family say about you?' Therefore, Judas went and hung himself. Up to now he is in torment where he is in hell. He will never have peace.

We cannot entertain the suggestion of suicide from anyone; not from the devil, yourself or anyone else in person or online. It is never right, and God will never lead you to do that.

Concerning Judas, Matthew Henry said, "He throws himself into the fire to avoid the flame; but miserable is the case when a man must go to hell for ease."[7] Miserable, he said, when a man must go to hell for ease. There is no ease in hell. Suicide only makes it worse. We cannot avoid the flame by jumping into the fire.

I am angry when I see so many taking their lives, being deceived, and thinking that it will be ok afterwards. I am afraid that like Judas, they are throwing themselves into eternal hell. There must be so much regret in hell by those who have been deceived into taking their own lives.

What must you do if you are under strain, pain and pressure? Go to those who can help you out of your problem. Go to a pastor, a professional counsellor, a respected person in the community or someone you know who loves you. Tell them about your challenges, and that you have been

---

[7] Matthew Henry, *An Exposition of the Old and New Testament*, (New York: Robert Carter and Brothers, 1865), 276

considering suicide. You need help. Don't isolate yourself; please tell someone. Live, and don't die. Life is a gift from God. Don't put out your own candle; let it shine. It is possible to shine even brighter after a dark season. Many have been resurrected from seasons of suicidal thoughts. You can too.

Chapter 5

To Be Saved Or Not To Be

There are millions of people who honestly believe that they are saved, but are not. They genuinely believe that they are on their way to Heaven but are not. They are deceived into a false sense of salvation and heavenly inheritance. A lot of people can be sincere about something but in reality this thing can be wrong. So it is with many who think they are saved but who may not be.

I am not the one who determines who is saved and who is not; I am not the standard for salvation. The Bible clearly states what one must do in order to be saved. It is unambiguous, and if one does not do what the word of God says, it is impossible to enter the kingdom of heaven, regardless of what other qualifications we may have or how pious we may be.

On that matter, this is what Jesus said, "...verily, verily, I say unto thee, Except a man be born again, he cannot see the kingdom of God" (John 3:3). The text says he cannot even 'see it', far less being able to enter into it. This is the number one qualification for entering into the kingdom of

God. You 'must' be born again. To be born again speaks of a new life, and in that new life one accepts Jesus as his personal and only Saviour. He is the one who died on the cross in our place. He bore our sins and it is only through Him that we can be saved from eternity in hell. We ask God to forgive us of our sins and Christ to come into our lives to be Master and Lord. We must then obey His word and do what He says. We must repent and be baptized and continue in His teaching, the Bible.

Without that we cannot be saved. It is not just going to church, giving and serving, taking communion and living well with neighbors that save a person, regardless of the Christian denomination they belong to. No, we must first make it right with God by genuinely repenting from our sins. We must ask Him to pardon us and we have to commit our lives to follow Him daily until we leave this earth. It is the whole new way of doing life.

This new life comes from the new birth and then and there we become His children. We must be regenerated and this regeneration is a gift from God. As Ephesians 2:8-9 says, "For by grace are ye saved through faith; and that not of yourselves: *it is* the gift of God: Not of works, lest any man should boast." You don't work to get it; you receive it from God. Jesus has done the work by dying on the cross for you and me. Now all we have to do is receive it by faith. If you work for it, then it is not a gift but payment for work you did. And if you work for it you will have the right to boast. But we cannot boast before God. Thereafter, we must live the way He says. We must not be afraid to identify with Him publicly either. If we deny Him, He will deny us.

Salvation is too important for God to have us pay for it. It is the most important human right. Therefore God has made it possible for all to access it free of charge. This is the most basic human right; no work is needed. All we need is faith in the grace of God, and we can all believe. On the other hand not all can work. If we depend only on our works, then we are disregarding the blood that Jesus shared on Calvary for our sins and the fact that it is 'by grace.'

Understanding Biblical Grace in reference to Salvation

The great blessing of salvation and eternal life is because of the grace of God. Without the grace of God we could have never been saved. So I believe that the doctrine of grace is one of the greatest in the Bible. As a matter of fact the Bible says, "For the law was given by Moses, *but* grace and truth came by Jesus Christ" (John 1:17).

Under the Old Testament they received law; under the New Testament we receive grace. Jesus is greater than Moses. Moses represents the law, Jesus represents grace. The law shows us our sins; grace helps us get rid of our sins.

The issue being addressed here is the incorrect application of grace, or the wrong teaching about grace. Some people believe that because we are under grace, we can sin freely without consequence for our actions. But the Bible clearly connects grace to living righteously. "For the grace of God that bringeth salvation hath appeared to all men, Teaching us that, denying ungodliness and worldly lusts, we should live soberly, righteously, and godly, in this present world;" (Titus 2:11-12).

Biblical grace does not encourage us to sin. It teaches us to live holy, denying ungodliness and worldly lusts. Paul makes the argument in Romans while talking to the Gentiles who had come in covenant through grace, that they should be careful how they live because they are there as a result of God's grace. He said they were grafted in. "Thou wilt say then, The branches were broken off, that I might be graffed in. Well; because of unbelief they were broken off, and thou standest by faith. Be not highminded, but fear: For if God spared not the natural branches, *take heed* lest he also spare not thee," (Romans 11:19-21). He says because of Israel's unbelief God cast them out even though they were the natural branches. The Gentiles were the grafted branches; that is they came in by grace. It is easier for a grafted branch to be broken off than the natural branch. Therefore, because we are there because of grace, we should be more careful and more appreciative of what Jesus has done for us.

It is like we committed a crime and we were supposed to die for that crime, but grace was granted unto us. Should we now go and commit more crimes? No. We should try our best to live in a way that is pleasing to the One who has shown us such grace. This is what Paul, the apostle of grace, says again about the matter; "What shall we say then? Shall we continue in sin, that grace may abound? God forbid. How shall we, that are dead to sin, live any longer therein?" (Romans 6:1-2)

Paul asks the question; shall we continue in sin that we might see more grace? And he answered it in this manner, 'God forbid, of course not. Don't even think about it. How shall we who have been set free want to go back into sin?' Some people believe the more sin we commit the more grace we will see, but I disagree. The more sin we practice is the more we don't appreciate grace and the more we abuse grace. Grace does not give license for people to practice immoralities. Grace is available for if we make a mistake, not when we make a mistake. By the way, the grace of God can keep us from falling, for "…greater is he that is within you, than he that is within the world" (1 John 4:4).

Paul says that we 'cannot continue in sin'. Our lives have been changed. Our goal is to glorify God in our mortal bodies and in all that we do. We seek to live as Jesus lived upon this earth. 2 Corinthians 5:17 says, "Therefore if any man *be* in Christ, *he is* a new creature: old things are passed away; behold, all things are become new." In Romans 6:6 we read, "…henceforth we should not serve sin." We are servants of righteousness, not of sin. Christ is our leader, not the devil nor the flesh. I like the way the People's New Testament puts it; "God forbid. The answer is emphatic. The thought is abhorrent, and the thing impossible from the very nature of the Christian life. The Christian life begins with a death to sin."[1]

Salvation which comes by God's grace gives us grace not to want to sin and grace to live in victory over sin.

Deception about 'Once Saved Always Saved'

This is a doctrinal stance of some of our Christian churches, 'Once saved always saved.' In addressing this subject, we need to hear what the Bible says and not what our churches or traditions or organizations teach. This teaching has been around for centuries, and many good church organizations have accepted this false doctrine without carefully looking at it scripturally. Doctrines are not formed by good arguments but by the teachings of scripture. So we will look at some of the scriptures and at reasons employed by the proponents of this doctrine. We will find out whether their arguments can

---

[1] B. W. Johnson, *The People's New Testament* –Romans, (Nashville: Gospel Advocate Co., 1891)

withstand the scrutiny of scripture. As I said, this teaching is very popular, even among gospel preaching churches, perhaps in your very church. But we are mature enough to look at both sides of the coin.

There are basically ten different views put forward on this teaching that once someone is saved once, he remains saved. The first is that 'Once one is saved he cannot backslide. If he backslides it means he was never saved.' In support of this doctrine Henry Clarence Thiessen says, "If a man habitually lives in sin, we conclude that he has never been saved."[2]

I totally disagree with this statement. I believe that if a man is saved he will live like a saved man. But if he backslides then he will start living again that old life that he first lived and, according to scripture, he will be worse than before. In 2 Peter 2:20-22, Peter says the following,

> For if after they have escaped the pollutions of the world through the knowledge of the Lord and Saviour Jesus Christ, they are again entangled therein, and overcome, the latter end is worse with them than the beginning. For it had been better for them not to have known the way of righteousness, than, after they have known *it,* to turn from the holy commandment delivered unto them. But it is happened unto them according to the true proverb, The dog *is* turned to his own vomit again; and the sow that was washed to her wallowing in the mire

[2] Henry Clarence Thiessen, *Lectures in Systematic Theology,* (Grand Rapids: William B. Eerdmans Pub. Co., 1989), page 297

'If after they have escaped the pollution of this world' he states. This refers to people who were once saved but turned their backs on their profession of faith. They turned away from Christ and went back into sin. Their lives become worse than before they knew God. The scripture says plainly, "It had been better for them not to have known the way of righteousness, than, after they have known *it,* to turn from the holy commandment delivered unto them." So there is no doubt that they were saved. The truth is that they backslid and returned to their old sinful habits. They forsook the Lord and they abandoned their salvation.

Let us examine a couple more scriptures on this point. Hebrews 10:26-27 says, "For if we sin wilfully after that we have received the knowledge of the truth, there remaineth no more sacrifice for sins, But a certain fearful looking for of judgment and fiery indignation, which shall devour the adversaries." The Bible says, 'if we sin wilfully *after* we have received the knowledge of the truth.' Isn't this plainly stating that we can come to a place where we can turn back to our former lives, the lives before we knew Christ? If we die in that condition we are not going to be saved, but receive a fiery indignation, which shall devour the adversaries.

There are many other scriptures, but let us turn to some of the scriptures that are used to support this false doctrine of irrevocable salvation. "For the gifts and calling of God are without repentance," (Romans 11:29). This is used to state that when He gives His gift of salvation He does not take it back. 'Without repentance' means not to be repented of.

There are some of God's promises that are not subject to condition, and there are others which are subject to conditions. Salvation is subject to conditions. If you follow Christ and remain steadfast you will have eternal life, not if you started and turned back. The true interpretation of this text above, according to B. W. Johnson, is "God does not change His purposes or fail to keep His covenant. What He has promised concerning Israel will be fulfilled."[3]

Again the proponents of this doctrine say that God does not change His mind about people. But let us tour the line of that argument. Let us prove that this argument is neither biblical nor sound.

God had given to Job wealth, blessings and then all was taken away except his wife. God had given him health and that too was taken away. And what did Job say? "Then Job arose, and rent his mantle, and shaved his head, and fell down upon the ground, and worshipped, And said, Naked came I out of my mother's womb, and naked shall I return thither: the LORD gave, and the LORD hath taken away; blessed be the name of the LORD" (Job 1:20-21). So Job said God gives and God takes away. He gave us life, and He can take it away whenever He wants.

The parable of the talents suggests that the Lord gives and the Lord takes away. Matthew 25:28 says, "Take therefore the talent from him, and give *it* unto him which hath ten talents." But the text does not just say take it from him. Remember also that it was given to him by his lord but because he refused to use it, his lord took it from him. Not only that, for the text says, "And cast ye the unprofitable servant into outer darkness: there shall be weeping and gnashing of teeth" (Matthew 25:30). The Bible called him an unprofitable servant. He was a child of God who did his own thing. So the belief that God does not take back what He has given to us is hereto proven silly.

If He is God He must have power to give and to take. If He cannot give and take then He is not God. The God of

---

[3] Johnson, *The People's New Testament*

Heaven and earth can do whatsoever He wants even when we cannot comprehend why. All we should say is that the God of all the earth does right.

Another text which is close to the heart of those who preach the 'once saved always saved unconditionally' doctrine, is John 10:27-30. "My sheep hear my voice, and I know them, and they follow me: And I give unto them eternal life; and they shall never perish, neither shall any *man* pluck them out of my hand. My Father, which gave *them* me, is greater than all; and no *man* is able to pluck *them* out of my Father's hand. I and *my* Father are one."

I agree fully that no one can take us out of the hand of God. No external forces can but we can remove ourselves from His hand. A sheep can walk out of the sheepfold. A sheep can follow another voice by choice. Salvation does not prevent or remove from us the power of choice. Even after we are saved we still have the ability to go astray and back into the world. Salvation does not immunize us from the ability to backslide. If we stay in the fold the enemy cannot touch us, but the truth is we have the free-will and ability to leave the fold. And sadly, many who were once there have left.

The argument using John 10:27-30 to defend the 'once saved always saved' doctrine, is held by people of high esteem, such as Stanley J. Grenz. He says, "Those who forsook the faith may someday return to the faith, because the indwelling spirit will complete his saving mission. Or they may never repent from their apostasy, revealing therefore that they were never genuinely converted."[4]

When one forsakes faith, does the Holy Spirit still dwell in him in his backslidden condition? My answer is no. If

[4] Stanley J. Grenz, *Theology for the Community of God,* (Grand Rapids, MI: William B. Eerdmans Pub Co., 1994), 455

you are a backslider, it means that the Holy Spirit no longer lives in you. If He is in you then you are not a backslider. Grenz states that if they never repent from their apostasy, it means that they were never saved. Apostasy means that you have abandoned your faith, that you left the faith you *once practiced*. You cannot be an apostate if you never had it. You cannot come out from something you were never in. So these people were saved.

Hebrews 6:4-6 says,

> For *it is* impossible for those who were once enlightened, and have tasted of the heavenly gift, and were made partakers of the Holy Ghost, And have tasted the good word of God, and the powers of the world to come, If they shall fall away, to renew them again unto repentance; seeing they crucify to themselves the Son of God afresh, and put *him* to an open shame.

So these people were made partakers of the Holy Ghost. They had a taste of the world to come. The scripture says it is impossible to renew them again, seeing they have crucified to themselves Christ afresh. They were saved but backslid and got to a place where they became apostate. They can no longer be saved. They once were but they lost their salvation of their own volition. God didn't take it. They gave it up and returned to a life of sin and condemnation.

Dake's commentary on Hebrews 4:6 says,

> How can they fall away from the experiences of v 4-5 if they never did have them? The language is past tense and factual, so it

cannot be denied that the ones referred to did at one time have these experiences; to fall aside; apostatize; fall away. It means to throw overboard all faith in the experiences of the gospel and deny them. Men are here warned that such is possible.

Let us look at some more scriptures that I believe prove further that the teaching of 'once saved always saved' is dangerous and misleading. On that issue Jesus says, "Remember Lot's wife" (Luke 17:32). It is one of the shortest verses in the Bible yet so powerful. Of all the men and women of the Bible the only one Jesus says to remember is Lot's wife. One must ask the question, why? Jesus had been encouraging His disciples to be faithful no matter what happened. He had encouraged them not to turn back. Then He proceeded to give them an example of someone who turned back and lost her blessing. She was saved out of Sodom before God destroyed Sodom. She was on the way to safety. God told them not to look or turn back. But see what happened.

And while he lingered, the men laid hold upon his hand, and upon the hand of his wife, and upon the hand of his two daughters; the LORD being merciful unto him: and they brought him forth, and set him without the city. And it came to pass, when they had brought them forth abroad, that he said, Escape for thy life; look not behind thee, neither stay thou in all the plain; escape to the mountain, lest thou be consumed (Genesis 19:16-17).

The instructions were clear among them: don't look back. But let us read Genesis 19:26; "But his wife looked back from behind him, and she became a pillar of salt."

Jesus warns us using this particular story to tell us that after we have been saved we ought not to turn back. Don't be like Lot's wife. She was saved, on her way to a place of safety but she turned back. 'Remember Lot's wife'.

Another passage, Jude 1:5 says "I will therefore put you in remembrance, though ye once knew this, how that the Lord, having saved the people out of the land of Egypt, afterward destroyed them that believed not." The Lord saved them, and afterwards He destroyed them for their unbelief. Jude says we must remember that. It means that these examples should encourage us to persevere instead of turning back. As the text plainly shows, once saved is not always saved.

The Lord, talking to the seven churches in the book of Revelation, from chapter 2 to chapter 3, warns His church, asking them to take heed to what He says. There is a common thread that runs through all messages to the churches: 'they that endure to the end shall be saved.' It means that if you don't endure to the end you will not be saved. Jesus encouraged the churches to be faithful unto death, and they would receive a crown of life. If we are not faithful to the end there will be no reward.

In Exodus the Bible states,

> And Moses returned unto the LORD, and said, Oh, this people have sinned a great sin, and have made them gods of gold. Yet now, if thou wilt forgive their sin; and if not, blot me, I pray thee, out of thy book which thou hast written. And the LORD said unto Moses, Whosoever hath sinned

against me, him will I blot out of my book
(Exodus 32:31-33).

What a prayer. It was a prayer with much faith, that God would hear and forgive His people for their sins. Moses made a great bargain here. He told God that if He did not forgive the people, that his name should be blotted out of the book. Now some ask, 'what book?' I believe it is the book of life, where the names of those who are saved are written. If that is true then that name can be removed, based on the text quoted from Exodus.

Some have ventured to reason that the text refers to the book of the living on earth. I have never read in the Bible that God has such a book, that when He kills someone on earth He then removes their name. In the book of Revelation we read of the Book of Life though. "He that overcometh, the same shall be clothed in white raiment; and I will not blot out his name out of the book of life, but I will confess his name before my Father, and before his angels" (Revelation 3:5). The verse says 'He that overcometh I will not blot out His name out of the book of life.' So there is a book of life with the names of the saints and if we turn from following Christ, our names will be blotted out. It sounds harsh, but it is in the Bible. If I had my way, I would change it so that some of my friends who are backslidden could be saved. However it is not what we want, but what the Word of God says.

We can keep on talking and quoting scriptures to either support or oppose the doctrine. Most of the scriptures used by the proponents of once saved always saved, are taken out of context, sometimes saying something totally different from what it really says. At times I wonder why good men teach this whether or not they accept it; regardless of the reason, it gives people license to sin. That kind of doctrine would put many souls in jeopardy of eternal hell. Many are drowning in a lifestyle of sin, and they say 'My pastor says I can never lose my salvation. It may be on my death bed but I will come back to God.' Many such persons known to us never came back.

Chapter 6

Deception In The Church About Discipline

Discipline is defined in the Merriam-Webster dictionary as punishment; training that corrects, molds, or perfects the mental faculties or moral character; control gained by enforcing obedience or order.[1]

There are many church leaders today who do not discipline their members. They can be involved in sexual sins or any number of immoral sins, yet there is no discipline. How is this happening in the church of Jesus Christ today? I can only speculate.

In some cases, if the leadership itself is living in sin, then it does not have the moral authority to discipline anyone. There are situations where some members know about the sins of the leaders. In such cases the leaders cannot discipline for fear of being exposed. So the church of the Lord becomes worse than a worldly club. At least in those clubs there is a measure of discipline.

---

[1] https://www.merriam-webster.com/dictionary/discipline

Another reason some don't discipline is because they want to maintain a large congregation. They are afraid that if they discipline that these members will leave their church and find another. But woe unto us if all we are concerned about is having a large, undisciplined group of people. What we should be doing is preparing people for heaven, not for ourselves and certainly not for hell. If there is no discipline then most probably it is not the Lord's church, for in the church of the Lord there is discipline of the highest order. In the kingdom of darkness anything goes.

The scripture has much to say about discipline or the lack thereof. Paul says,

> Know ye not that the unrighteous shall not inherit the kingdom of God? Be not deceived: neither fornicators, nor idolaters, nor adulterers, nor effeminate, nor abusers of themselves with mankind, Nor thieves, nor covetous, nor drunkards, nor revilers, nor extortioners, shall inherit the kingdom of God. And such were some of you: but ye are washed, but ye are sanctified, but ye are justified in the name of the Lord Jesus, and by the Spirit of our God" (1 Corinthians 6:9-11).

Paul gave a long list of sins, stating that people who practice such sins shall not inherit the kingdom of God. He said further, that there was a time we were involved in such, but God has washed us from these sins. We are now sanctified; therefore we should not go back to these sins or any sins whatsoever. If we do, we shall not enter the kingdom of God.

A further reference to the Bible must be made on the matter of indiscipline in the church. In 1 Corinthians 5:1-5, Paul writes,

> It is reported commonly *that there is* fornication among you, and such fornication as is not so much as named among the Gentiles, that one should have his father's wife. And ye are puffed up, and have not rather mourned, that he that hath done this deed might be taken away from among you. For I verily, as absent in body, but present in spirit, have judged already, as though I were present, *concerning* him that hath so done this deed, In the name of our Lord Jesus Christ, when ye are gathered together, and my spirit, with the power of our Lord Jesus Christ, To deliver such an one unto Satan for the destruction of the flesh, that the spirit may be saved in the day of the Lord Jesus.

What we have read here is one of the worst sins one can find in the church, in that a brother was living with his father's wife. Paul said that one would not even hear such sin among the unbelievers. But the amazing thing to note is that the church took no action on those who had committed such a sin. And Paul seemed to be angry with the church for not taking action. He said persons were puffed up, rather than being in mourning. And then he said 'he that hath this deed might be taken away from you.' In other words, you cannot have a brother or sister who practices sin among you and behave like nothing happened. You would be turning a blind eye to the sin.

In that particular case Paul recommends the worse kind of excommunication. He said 'deliver such an one unto Satan for the destruction of the flesh, that the spirit may be saved in the day of the Lord Jesus.' What a scandal in the church, what a sin. But the punishment is very severe. Paul seems to suggest that when you hand him over to the devil for punishment, chances are that he might see his error and repent. The text says for the destruction of the body; that the devil might harm his body with sickness or disease, that he might call on God for mercy.

We must take this story further. Paul says, "Purge out therefore the old leaven, that ye may be a new lump, as ye are unleavened. For even Christ our passover is sacrificed for us:" (1 Corinthians 5:7). So he calls sin in our midst leaven and we need to get the sin out.

He goes on to make another strong statement about discipline in the church. Now, we must note that this is the New Testament, and the same Paul who spoke so much about grace is writing this.

> I wrote unto you in an epistle not to company with fornicators: Yet not altogether with the fornicators of this world, or with the covetous, or extortioners, or with idolaters; for then must ye needs go out of the world. But now I have written unto you not to keep company, if any man that is called a brother be a fornicator, or covetous, or an idolater, or a railer, or a drunkard, or an extortioner; with such an one no not to eat (1 Corinthians 5:9-11)

He is saying that we must not even eat with a brother or sister who is living in sin. We must let them know that we are disappointed with this type of lifestyle and so is Jesus Christ. They need to repent and forsake these sins in order to have fellowship with the church. You may be saying that was just one extreme case and that is why Paul made such a statement. Well, let us look at what Ephesians 5:11-12 says; "And have no fellowship with the unfruitful works of darkness, but rather reprove *them.* For it is a shame even to speak of those things which are done of them in secret."

He says we must not have any fellowship with people who are in church and practicing evil works. He says we must reprove these people. Again we read from the pen of Apostle Paul, "And if any man obey not our word by this epistle, note that man, and have no company with him, that he may be ashamed. Yet count *him* not as an enemy, but admonish *him* as a brother" (2 Thessalonians 3:14-15). If there are some in the church who will reject the words of God, we must mark them and have no company with those persons. Paul says it is so that they would be ashamed. Sometimes as leaders we are afraid to discipline people because some say that we are embarrassing them. Our goal must be to restore, but the nature of sin always makes us ashamed.

Even from the beginning when Adam and Eve committed the first sin, their only sin, God came, and although He forgave them, He disciplined them. They were put out of the garden. He put Cherubims with swords to prevent them from taking of the tree of life. They had to work hard from that time on. There was punishment for their sin. The church of Jesus Christ must have discipline.

In closing this section, a few more scriptures will be quoted so that we might be clear as to what the Bible says on the subject. Paul again warns Timothy, who is a pastor and leader over churches that he would have to take some decisions which may not be popular with some in the church.

He says to him in 1 Timothy 1:19-20, "Holding faith, and a good conscience; which some having put away concerning faith have made shipwreck: Of whom is Hymenaeus and Alexander; whom I have delivered unto Satan, that they may learn not to blaspheme."

Paul says he delivered Hymenaeus and Alexander to the devil. Now 2 Timothy 2:17-18 tells us a little more about these characters. It seems they were believers who went astray into heresy. One of the false areas of teaching was that the resurrection was already passed, and that false doctrine caused many to lose the faith. Let us look at exactly what the Word says in 2 Timothy 2:17-18. "And their word will eat as doth a canker: of whom is Hymenaeus and Philetus; Who concerning the truth have erred, saying that the resurrection is past already; and overthrow the faith of some."

So Paul put these people out of the church because sin begets more sin. If you don't remove sins that you know of, it quickly multiplies. When you cover up sins they hatch faster. Sin hinders the church from moving forward. It is like the sons of Eli going to fight with the enemy, when their lifestyles were like that of the enemy. It is like the devils casting out devils. That cannot work. The house of God must not look like the house of the devil.

Chapter 7

The Deception Of Materialism

Materialism has a very subtle deception because of the needs and nature of man, as well as the frequency and bombardment of advertisements or promotion of material things. Let us first define materialism. "The word 'materialism' is used in various ways. Its most popular usage is in reference to people guilty of greed and avarice. A 'materialist' is someone whose life revolves around his material possessions.

> The other major definition of 'materialism' is used in a philosophical and technical sense, referring to those who reduce or limit reality to material objects. Their creed is 'Everything that is, is material.' By this they mean anything not of a material nature does not exist, and is only a figment of man's imagination. Thus God, by definition, does not exist. Man himself is only a material machine with no soul or

spiritual essence. Everything that is man
is material.[1]

I want to deal with both aspects of materialism as
explained above, for both forms are deceptive. Let us first
look at its reference to greed for earthly material things. Greed
and prosperity are not the same and one can be prosperous
without being greedy for stuff. There is nothing wrong with
wealth if it is gained the right way and used for the right
purposes. Furthermore God wants us to be wealthy but He
does not want us to get wealth at the expense of our soul.
And added to that, our wealth should be used to bring glory
to God.

Materialism is so deceptive it is one of the subjects that
the Bible warned us about the most. Jesus said,

> Lay not up for yourselves treasures upon
> earth, where moth and rust doth corrupt,
> and where thieves break through and steal:
> But lay up for yourselves treasures in heaven,
> where neither moth nor rust doth corrupt,
> and where thieves do not break through nor
> steal: For where your treasure is, there will
> your heart be also" (Matthew 6:19-21).

Jesus does not say we should not have treasures. It is ok
with God if we have. But when we do, it must be used for the
furtherance of the kingdom of God.

The problem with many of us and materialism is that
we covet it at the expense of our souls and even our family

---

[1] Robert A. Morey, *The New Atheism and the Erosion of Freedom*,
(Las Vegas, NV: Christian Scholars Press, 2000), 90

life. Many persons who were at one time strong in the faith get busy seeking stuff to the point that they are not even in church any more. There are some who seek to buy everything they can, even when they don't have the money (for things can be purchased on credit), to the point that they cannot even fulfill their basic responsibilities to God with their money. I refer to the requirement of giving God a tenth, a tithe. They are unable to fulfill that requirement because nearly all of it goes towards paying for a materialistic lifestyle.

Sometimes, because we are trying to live material-based lifestyles, we have to work two and three jobs. This takes us out of our homes for most of the month, or we may be home, but too tired or busy for our family and so family life falls apart. At times marriages end in divorce because we don't have time for our family. We are too busy trying to be better than our neighbours, materially.

God hates this. 1 Timothy 6:10 says, "For the love of money is the root of all evil: which while some coveted after, they have erred from the faith, and pierced themselves through with many sorrows." Sorrows of divorce, the sorrows of children backsliding, sorrows of ill health, sorrows of worry and so many other sorrows are caused by materialism.

It is easy to fall into the trap of materialism.

> Our culture oozes with toxic materialism.
> A lying spirit tells the masses that more money and better things are the two tickets we need for admission to the life we desire. If we have the right labels, the new gadgets, the best techno-toys, the latest luxury cars, the nicest custom-built houses, and the

fattest 401k's, then we'll be happy, secure
and significant.[2]

If you are not strong and disciplined, there is a social
pressure that compels you to enter the web of materialism.
It is so easy to fall into the trap. You don't have to possess
the cash to get the item that you see advertised on television
every hour or so, or what you see at the stores. You can buy it
right away and pay later. There are some items you can have
now and make your first payment a whole year later. They
allow us to consume before we pay. But we must open our
eyes and remember that we will have to pay. Before we know
it, in five years time we would have taken so much credit that
one job cannot cover the debts.

> According to a recent article, 60 percent of
> workers under the age of thirty have already
> cashed in their retirement. A whopping 70
> percent of them have no money whatsoever
> in cash reserves. Nevertheless, they keep
> spending and charging. Although the
> generation of twenty-and thirty-somethings
> has many positive traits, one of the negatives
> is the spirit of entitlement. I deserve it. Life
> is short. And I want it now.[3]

They have not worked for it, yet they believe they deserve
it. They compare themselves to persons who have worked
for forty years and want to own the same valuable things

---

[2] Craig Groeschel, *Soul Detox: Clean Living in a Contaminated
World*, (Grand Rapids, Michigan: Zondervan, 2012), 164

[3] Groeschel, *Soul Detox,* 165

they see, though they have only just started in the work force. So they end up mortgaging their future, all because of materialism.

Materialism is one of the most effective things used by Satan to drive people to himself because it seems quite normal and legal. Yet thousands have been driven away from church and God because they have to work to try to make the extra money to pay for a particular lifestyle that God did not approve of. Many Christians are busy, but it is not in working for God but to pay for what they have consumed on their own lust.

What is the solution? I suggest one try their best to stay off and pay off debts. Sell some of the things which are not necessary to clear your debts. Live within your means. Don't let society decide what is right for you. The Word of God says what is right and wrong. Realize that this is a spiritual struggle, not just a physical one. The devil is out for your souls and he doesn't want you to be a good steward of what God has given you. Change your lifestyle and do it now.

Let us now spend some time on the other definition of materialism, where it is used in a philosophical and technical sense. This belief states that anything that is not of a material nature does not exist.

It is hard to believe that some learnt men do not want to admit that there is an unseen but real world. This world is even more powerful than our seen world. And, if we would be honest, many of us have had encounters with spiritual beings. Now spiritual beings as used here, does not just refer to God, for many have had encounters with devils. They have sought the devil for power, protection, wealth and more and have received things, albeit at the expense of their souls. Also, there are many credible testimonies of people who have had encounters with God or angels in some form.

There are millions of people living now who have had dreams and visions. Some have been given direction and even healing in these visions and dreams. Now, are we to say that there is nothing called a dream because we never have one? There was a time when we could not fathom that someone could speak from within the United States and be answered right away by someone in Australia. But now we know that is possible. There are many things we may not know now, not see now and may never experience, but that does not mean they do not exist. There is more than what we see. There is more than just material. There is a spiritual, non-material dimension in life.

Chapter 8

Deception And The New Age Movement

The New Age movement is so subtle that we need to be educated about it so that we do not become deceived. You see, New Age teaching is everywhere. It is not just a denomination or a particular organization or nation or group. The movement finds itself mixed in with organizations and churches, including Christian churches as well as cults. Therefore, we need to know who and what it is because it may already be in our midst and having negative influences.

Dr Selwyn Stevens says "The New Age doesn't wish to reject the Christian church – it seeks to absorb it and change it from within. It has been far more successful than most Christians realise, especially in the last decade."[1]

This statement about trying to bring everyone under a one world government and religion is exactly what the antichrist will seek to do. So those who are seeking to do that are already working for him.

---

[1] Selwyn Stevens, *The New Age: The Old Lie in a New Package*, (New Zealand: Jubilee Resources International Inc,2002), 6

Although the New Age practitioners as a whole do not have an established set of beliefs, there are some that we can identify. They believe that they are God. Speaking about Christmas, they say "Instead of commemorating the advent of 'God with us' we attempt to recover the God who is us. The birth of Jesus is merely an occasion to reflect on our own potential as gods and goddesses in the making. As Joseph Campbell puts it, we are all incarnations of God – only some of us have not yet realized it."[2]

They don't believe in the creator God who made all things, them included. No, they believe we are all gods, except that some of us do not know it yet. So one of their goals is to enlighten humanity to the point that a person can recognize that he or she is God. But, isn't it ironic that God has to be enlightened to know that He is all powerful, all seeing, all knowing. It is strange that God does not know that He is God and there must be a process before He can know this. This may indeed sound strange to us, even moronic, but there are many who believe it.

"New Age theology exchanges the personal God of Christianity for an impersonal Force; Principle, or Consciousness. Humans can tap into this Force through a change in consciousness and realize their own divinity, as did Jesus and other mystical masters. But there is no need for the forgiveness of sin because there is no sin to forgive and no personal, loving God to provide a sacrifice for it. An impersonal God cannot love anyone."[3]

If we are gods it is obvious we don't have sin, for gods

---

[2] Douglas Groothuis, *Christianity that Counts; Being a Christian in a Non-Christian World*, (Grand Rapids, MI: Baker Books, 1994), 183-184

[3] Groothuis, *Christianity That Counts*, 184

don't sin. Can you see the deception in this movement? People can even deny that they can sin or have sin. So these people are saying that if you have murdered people, raped, abused, caused people to suffer unjustly, bomb innocent people, that is not sin. What deception!

> Christianity teaches that humanity's problem is that we have rebelled against God and have thereby broken our relationship with Him. The New Age movement teaches, on the other hand, that there is nothing we can possibly do to sever the connection that exists between us and the divine Oneness. Our problem is that of ignorance, say the New Ager, not rebellion. We have forgotten who we are in our true selves, which is one with the Universal Self. The goal of yoga, meditation, and other mind expanding techniques is to experience that Oneness.[4]

So according to them, we never fell from anything - sin did not enter the world. So, it makes the Bible a liar. However, the Bible says that we "all have sinned and come short of the glory of God" (Romans 3:23). But there is something I want you to notice in that teaching, which is, the problem is that of ignorance.

Many Christian preachers today are preaching a similar theology, just with a slight twist. They are saying that because we are saved, God has taken care of our past, present and future sins, so we don't even have to confess them. God has

---

[4] Dean Halverson, *The Illustrated Guide to World Religions*, (Bloomington, Minnesota: Bethany House Publishers, 2003), 176-177

taken care of that. It is just that some of us are ignorant about the power of God's grace. This is scriptural malpractice and has roots in New Age thinking.

The New Agers also believe in reincarnation, which states that, when you die, you come back to earth in another form. This is a dangerous concept. It is not funny when we are dealing with matters that have to deal with man's soul. But reincarnation sounds like a joke. Dying and coming back in another form, animals included? Imagine dying and returning as a goat, being slaughtered and eaten. Some meat would go to that person's blood stream and some I suppose would go to the toilet, and then what form would the person return in? This is great deception. The fact is that, man has a spirit and a soul and will have to face the judge of all the earth, God Almighty. Man would either be received into glory, or cast to the lake of fire, for after death is the judgment.

The New Ager is opened to all kinds of ungodly beliefs and they come from various backgrounds. "A New Age person might be a Hindu, Buddhist, Wiccan (witch) or an astrologer, channeler or parapsychologist. His or her cause might be 'deep ecology,' animal rights, holistic healing, or UFOs."[5] It is a mixture of everything, as long as you come together, to create a world of peace and prosperity.

Another New Age belief is that you can find assistance to getting in touch with who you really are. Here are the ways you can.

> New Agers encourage people to get in touch
> with their spirit guides who are able to assist
> them along their path of spiritual evolution
> and transformation. The various kinds

---

[5] Halverson, *The Illustrated Guide to World Religions*, 170

> of beings that can be contacted include
> Ascended Masters, disembodied spirits
> who lived in physical bodies at one time,
> UFOs, the spirits of animals, and angels.[6]

From our understanding of spiritual matters this in essence is introducing you to demonic spirits. They use terms as disembodied spirits (spirits that are without a body). In other words they are looking for a body to possess.

When you join these movements you open your life to all forms of demonic spirits and you become a toy, tool or messenger of Satan. They use your body to do the work of Satan. The angels they refer to are not the angels of God, for God's angels do not help people who speak against God, or deny that there is a God who is the creator of all and that we are all subject to Him. So the angels spoken about by the New Age movement are fallen angels, demons, and wicked spirits. New Age gurus encourage persons to call upon those spirits for help and guidance. Friend, the best guide for you is the Holy Spirit.

Freemasonry in a New Age

The following is a quote from a former Mason. "Masonry is an antichristian religion, and when Christians, especially Christian leaders join it, we should become alarmed."[7] Masonry does not claim to be a religion for a very good reason. If they claim to be a religion they would have to say which religion. By so doing many other religions would not

---

[6] Ibid, 179

[7] William Schnoebelen, *Masonry: Beyond The Light* (Chino, CA: Chick Publications, 1991), 21.

join them. It would also make it harder for the non-religious, the non-church-goer to join them.

The Masons are within many religions, and there are those who belong to no religion at all. So they prefer to say that they are an organization that exists to assist people and to make good men better. Masonry is a religion, but they don't want to let the outsider and the newly converted know which god they are truly serving. To be a religion does not necessarily mean that the one being served is the Creator of the world. The religion may have more than one god or they may have Satan as their god.

The following is what a former Mason said; "In the first degree (entered apprentice), the candidate is barely inside the Lodge door for his initiation when he is summarily challenged by the question, 'In whom do you put your trust?' His answer must be 'In God', otherwise, he is not allowed to proceed with the initiation ritual."[8] They must pledge their allegiance to a supreme being but that being is not the true God. They make the converts believe that it is the true God, but it is far from that.

The Masons accept any one who believes in any god. Therefore it cannot be the true God. The True God, the God of the Bible, has made it abundantly clear that we should not worship any other god but Him. If you are a worshipper of other gods, then God is not your god. Satan is your god. And all the other 'gods' are false gods under the power of Satan. William Schnoebelen, a former high degree Mason said, "Thus if you tell a Satanist that he cannot be a mason because his supreme being, the devil, isn't up to snuff, you are in violation of Masonic principles."[9]

---

[8] Schnoebelen, *Masonry Beyond The Light, 21*

[9] Schnoebelen, *Masonry Beyond The Light, 21*

In other words, a Satanist can have full membership in the lodge without renouncing Satan as his supreme god. So the idea that this is a good organization is false. Satanist, witchcraft workers, those of any religion, and those of no religion can all become members. The god who is acknowledged in the lodge is really who they refer to as the great architect of the universe. That is why they have many signs and symbols of architects such as the square and the compass, and of some other professions, which show that they are members of this secret, evil society.

Again there are all kinds of new ways and a multiplicity of options in the world today when it comes to religion and God. That after all is and has always been a strategy of Satan, that is, to provide so many different gods for so many different things that many feel compelled to explore and choose what fits their preference. In the Old Testament Israel was similarly led astray by often moving away from the one True God to follow the pagan gods around them. But just as most if not all of these religions died and only Jehovah God, the God of Abraham, Isaac and Jacob remained, so shall it come to pass in our modern day. It will come to pass that only the religion of Jehovah God, and His Son Jesus and His religion Christianity, will stand. Amen.

Chapter 9

Deception Of Culture

The ways people behave vary from place to place, but there are some behaviors that are rejected almost everywhere. The Merriam-Webster dictionary defines culture as 'the customary beliefs, social forms, and material traits of a racial, religious or social group.'[1]

Sadly many nations and people groups adopt cultures which are immoral. That is one of the biggest problems in the world today. These immoral practices bring hatred, curses and diseases among people. If we were to accept the teaching of the Bible and behave accordingly, our lives would be better spiritually, socially, physically and mentally.

We must be careful that we cultivate the right culture. Some of the things which have become culture for us include going to a movie that has much violence and listening to a comedy filled with obscene language. We fill our minds and spirits with curse words and violent actions and we say this is our culture.

We say nothing is wrong with the profane language we listen to at the movies, nor the nude parties we attend nor

---

[1] www.merriam-webster.com/dictionary/culture

the drinking of alcohol. We say this is part of culture. What does God call it: The way of the old life; walking in darkness. He says that the things that are done in darkness are even a shame to talk about (Ephesians 5:12). But we pay our money and go among unbelievers to listen to a comedy that would be laced with obscenity and we try to justify this by calling it culture. But I say that as long as your culture is contrary to the Word of God, you must reject it.

Craig Groeschel says,

> Movies, media and culture are not bad in themselves. But consuming spiritually toxic material from our culture without discernment can kill you. People in our culture don't have the same standards, priorities or responsibilities that we as Christians have. If pleasing God is not their focus, why should they care what they put in a movie, song, TV show, magazine, article or book?[2]

You see, the enemy is trying to kill us little by little. He will dilute the poison to make it palatable and contagious, and once we are hooked, it becomes difficult to break from the bad habit. The best thing is to never get into it in the first place. Culture must be based on truth, not in myth and evil practices.

Our culture has now become a violent culture. I believe that it all started with the breakdown in morality. We must have a clear code of morality, and it must be fair and just in order to have a peaceful and good society. And there must

---

[2] Groeschel, *Soul Detox*, 181

be punishment. It is not about just having laws, but the laws must be alive and well. They must be just and administered speedily.

But we must not just have, for instance, prison officers to deal with inmates. We must have counsellors, at least facilitators, who can speak and work with the prisoners every day. They must be taught the right way and shown the way forward. They should not just be imprisoned for a certain number of years. There must be restoration while they are incarcerated.

What you believe is what you will practice. So we must teach the truth in our culture, so that we will have the right outcome. Society must teach its people well. Bad teaching produces bad citizens and bad cultures.

Charles Colson and Anne Morse say,

> Laws will never be enough to stop crime. We must first address ourselves to culture: the ideas and attitudes of the elites who shape the way the people think. The philosophy of existentialism is false. Real morality is not man-made. Nor is it imposed on us merely be society. The source of true moral standards is God Himself.[3]

Many of the persons who commit crimes believe that the laws of the land are man-made and were implemented to keep some people subjugated. But if the laws are godly, then they are not offensive and no one should rebel against them. At times society is not the problem. But it may facilitate

---

[3] Charles Colson and Anne Morse, *Burden of truth,* (Wheaton, IL: Tyndale House, 1997), 146

the problem and is unable to stop it. The scripture says, "If the foundations be destroyed, what can the righteous do?" (Psalm 11:3). We must ensure that our foundation as nations is based on the Word of God, or else we will be deceived and even destroyed by our own culture.

Chapter 10

Man As Body, Soul And Spirit

Understanding the Makeup of Man

In 1 Thessalonians 5:23 and Hebrews 4:12 the Bible speaks of man having body, soul and spirit. To truly understand man we need to understand these three parts of man.

To properly comprehend something you need to understand what makes it what it is. We cannot expect an engine to function at its optimum if we don't put all the major parts in. We cannot truly understand mankind without looking at all the parts.

God is the one who created man. Therefore no one can definitively describe man like God can. In the Bible, God's word, God says who man is and what he is made up of.

The Minirth Guide to Christian Counselors, referring to the scripture earlier in 1 Thessalonians 5:23 says, "The reference is to the spiritual aspect of man; the psychological aspect of man, and, finally, the physical aspect."[1] Each part

---

[1] Frank Minirth, *The Minirth Guide for Christian Counselors*, (Nashville TN: B&H Publishing Group, 2003) 10-11

deals with a different aspect of man's life and his ability to reach different realms. The book continues to speak about the function of the soul.

> The soul is the psychological aspect of man. Psychiatrists and psychologists have focused their endeavors on this aspect of man. The hope has been to help individuals with confused minds, weak wills and labile emotions. The Bible focuses on these three functions of the soul. In Job 6:7 and Job 7:15, reference is made to the ability of the soul to choose (the will). In Psalms 139:14 and Proverbs 19:2, reference is made to the intellectual or knowing aspect of the soul (the mind). Finally in 2 Samuel 5:8 and Song of Solomon 1:7, reference is made to emotions as a function of the soul.[2]

We interact with God and the world with all three dimensions of our souls. For example a Christian can have emotional problems. On the other hand, he can reject a move of God because his mind may tell him this is not of God. Or his intellect may tell him that this is not how it ought to be done. Therefore all that we are must be subject to the will of God. Furthermore, we must go deeper than the flesh and the soul and allow God to deal with our spirits.

> Many problems could be avoided for the Christian if he just lived a life constantly as Christ wanted him to live. He would avoid

---

[2] Minirth, *The Minirth Guide for Christian Counselors*, 11-12

many things that cause guilt, anxiety and stress. Thus, the following question arises: if Christians have a new life and power within them at the time of conversion, why do they continue to have mental and emotional problems? One reason is that the mind is a part of the soul, not the spirit. The soul does not become new or have any change at the time of conversion; the spirit does. Only after a person has spent time in the word of God and in prayer, and in fellowship is the mind renewed in accordance with the will of God (Rom 12:1).[3]

We sin because, although we are saved, we still have our own will and at times we choose to do our will rather than God's will. Hence it is important that we know the Word and do what it says. We must feed our spirit with spiritual things, the things of God and not the things of the flesh. The fact that we have a sinful nature means that the possibility of sin is there. When we get saved the sinful nature is not eradicated. We must be mindful to not feed that old nature. Rather we should feed the new one, the one Christ gave us as His children through redemption. We are now children of God and He has given to us His divine nature as stated in 2 Peter 1:4.

---

[3] Minirth, *The Minirth Guide for Christian Counselors,* 13

Man Has a Body

Man needs to understand himself if he is to function properly. As stated earlier, there are three essential parts in man: body, soul and spirit. These parts help us to function in this world, in the spirit world and even in the world beyond death.

The subject of a tripartite human being is an area of various views. There are those who believe that man is just body and spirit. There are others who say that the words soul and spirit are used interchangeably, meaning the same thing.

There are those who don't even believe that God is the one who created man. But God did create man. The Bible tells us how He did it. We need to look deep into the scriptures to see what it says about the makeup of man. God has spoken on this matter. The first mention of man as body, soul and spirit is found in Genesis 2:7; "And the LORD God formed man *of* the dust of the ground, and breathed into his nostrils the breath of life; and man became a living soul."

The scripture here talks about God forming man out of the ground. He shaped man out of material he had previously created by His spoken word. Before man, God created everything by His spoken word. When it got to the creation of man God got involved in a very personal way, by forming man's body out of the dust of the ground. Although there is little disagreement in the Christian church about how the body of man came about, just for good measure, a few scriptures will be quoted.

> And the LORD God caused a deep sleep to fall upon Adam, and he slept: and he took one of his ribs, and closed up the flesh instead thereof; And the rib, which the LORD God had taken from man, made he

> a woman, and brought her unto the man.
> And Adam said, This *is* now bone of my
> bones, and flesh of my flesh: she shall be
> called Woman, because she was taken out
> of Man (Genesis 2:21-23).

Both Adam and Eve were made out of the same material, for she was taken out of Adam. The bodies of both male and female were hence taken from the ground. And that which came from the ground is the physical part which we can see, that is the body. It is of the earth.

The body is called an earthly house. This is what the Apostle Paul says in 2 Corinthians 5:1; "For we know that if our earthly house of *this* tabernacle were dissolved, we have a building of God, an house not made with hands, eternal in the heavens." So this body is for the earth. A house is used as a home and protection for whatever is inside of it. The house does not have life in itself. What is in the house gives it life. As soon as whatever is inside leaves, then there is no more life in the house.

This body of ours is for earthly function. It houses the soul and the spirit. As soon as the soul and the spirit leave the body, it becomes dead. What give the body life are the soul and the spirit within it. The body is an earthly house. For instance, the shell of a whelk (or what is known as a sea snail) is a house for the sea creature. After the whelk leaves the shell, the shell becomes lifeless. So is the body of man. Once what is inside is gone, it is lifeless. But what was inside goes on to live without the body in another world. Is the body important? It is very important for the functioning of this life.

Now the body is not evil, it is neither good nor bad. It is the life inside of it that determines what path it takes. This is what Paul says about the body; "I beseech you therefore, brethren, by the mercies of God, that ye present your bodies a living sacrifice, holy, acceptable unto God, *which is* your reasonable service" (Romans 12:1). It must be presented to God as holy. It indeed can be holy and acceptable to God. It depends on how it is controlled by its 'occupants' – the spirit and soul within.

The body is a tool, for good or for evil, for the use of God or of the devil. The occupant decides. God wants our bodies to be a place, not just for our spirits, but for His Holy Spirit to live and to do His work on earth through us. He wants to use us, but this body must be holy. The apostle says, "If a man therefore purge himself from these, he shall be a vessel unto honour, sanctified, and meet for the master's use, *and* prepared unto every good work" (2 Timothy 2:21). So God wants to use us as instruments in His hand, but that body and the life it contains must be clean.

This body must be used to minister to others. Jesus' body was used to bring glory to God. "Forasmuch then as Christ hath suffered for us in the flesh, arm yourselves likewise with the same mind: for he that hath suffered in the flesh hath ceased from sin; That he no longer should live the rest of *his* time in the flesh to the lusts of men, but to the will of God" (1 Peter 4:1-2).

Our bodies must not be servants of sin but of righteousness. There are people who will do whatsoever the enemy tells them to do. They are servants of the devil. But the Christian must use his body to serve God. As the Apostle Paul says,

> Let not sin therefore reign in your mortal body, that ye should obey it in the lusts thereof. Neither yield ye your members *as*

> instruments of unrighteousness unto sin:
> but yield yourselves unto God, as those that
> are alive from the dead, and your members
> *as* instruments of righteousness unto God
> (Romans 6:12-13).

Don't give your body as an instrument to be used by the devil. Rather, let your body be an instrument or a weapon in the hand of God against the enemy. It says 'yield' your body to God, not to Satan. You have the power to yield to whosoever you want to control your body. An elephant does not have to allow anyone to ride on its back, but it yields to allow even children to ride on it. It can run away, but it yields. We can yield either to God or to the devil. We have the power to allow our bodies to be used as a weapon against Satan or as a tool to do his work. Your body can be used as a weapon or a tool on either side. It depends on you.

Let every part of your body be a dangerous weapon against Satan: your tongue, your hands, to name a few. The enemy is afraid of a holy weapon, but takes advantage of an unholy weapon and keeps it in bondage. The sons of Sceva were not living holy and were trying to cast demons out of a man. The account reads, "And the evil spirit answered and said, Jesus I know, and Paul I know; but who are ye? And the man in whom the evil spirit was leaped on them, and overcame them, and prevailed against them, so that they fled out of that house naked and wounded" (Acts 19:15-16).

We must let our bodies be holy weapons like Paul's body was, that we might bring blessing to the world and not curses. The Bible says, "Therefore, brethren, we are debtors, not to the flesh, to live after the flesh. For if ye live after the flesh, ye shall die: but if ye through the Spirit do mortify the deeds of the body, ye shall live" (Romans 8:12-13).

Man Has a Soul

The soul is the life. Life is as mysterious as the soul itself. The soul is the self. The Zondervan Pictorial Encyclopedia of the Bible looking at etymology and the definition of the word 'soul', notes, "BDB provides no less than ten different meanings of the term, and it is suggested that its origin is to be found in the Akkad. *napasu* meaning "to get breath," "be broad," "extended" or perhaps from the related term *napistu* meaning "life" but sometimes used as "soul," "living being," "person."[4]

Let us bring the Trichotomous view of man into the picture. "Tricholomy comes from Greek tricha, 'three', and temno, 'to cut'. Hence man is a three-part being, consisting of body, soul and spirit. The soul and spirit are said to be different both in function and in substance. The body is seen as world-conscious, the soul as self-conscious and the spirit as God-conscious."[5]

The Holman Treasury of Key Bible Words put it beautifully. It says,

> Only people have the ability to reason and investigate the world. People alone have the privilege of knowing God in a personal way, sharing His wisdom and enjoying eternal life. Only mankind is threatened with the prospect of eternal torment for rejecting God, because all these things are made

[4] Merrill C. Tenny, *The Zondervan Pictorial Encyclopedia of the Bible,* (Grand Rapids, MI: Regency Reference Library, 1989), 496
[5] Paul P. Enns, *The Moody Handbook of Theology,* (Chicago: Moody Press, 2014), 307

> possible by God's creation of a man and
> woman with a soul.[6]

God took a personal interest in man when He was creating mankind. He took some time and shaped him. He breathed His Spirit into man personally so that man can, through his spirit, communicate with God, have fellowship with God, and God with man.

The soul is what identifies you. Every man has a soul. The soul is you. Let's go back to the text in Genesis 2:7 which was mentioned earlier, for that is where the doctrine of the body, soul and spirit was first mentioned. "And the LORD God formed man *of* the dust of the ground, and breathed into his nostrils the breath of life; and man became a living soul."

After God breathed into man's nostrils something supernatural happened. Life came into that body. He became a living soul. God performed divine chemistry. As He breathed into man's nostrils, life came into being. As God's breath hit the body a person was created, a soul came about. The spirit in the body birthed a soul, a person. When God breathed into man's body he became something that he was not before, a living soul. It was God's chemistry, God's power, God's ability and only He can create that way.

In Job 33:4, Job says, "The Spirit of God hath made me, and the breath of the Almighty hath given me life." What made you Job? The Spirit of God. His breath gave me life. So life comes from God. The soul comes from God. God is the one who made the body and God is the one who made

---

[6] Eugene E. Carpenter, *Holman Treasury of Key Bible Words; 200 Greek and 200 Hebrew words Defined and Explained,* (Nashville, TN: Holman Reference, 2000), 178

the soul and God is the one who gave the spirit. Man came from God, body, soul and spirit.

If you take sand, cement and water, and mixed them together at the right proportion, after the mixing you will not have sand, cement or water any more. Because of the chemistry you have a new entity called mortar, even though it is made up of sand, cement and water. The Spirit of God breathed into man brought forth a new entity, the soul. The soul can live without the body, but the body has no life without the soul. The soul is the life. The soul is you.

Now, even when your body dies and is buried, you can be identified in the afterlife without DNA evidence. Every man has his personal soul, and he is identified by his soul, even without the body. Moses had died for hundreds of years and was buried by God Himself. According to the book of Deuteronomy, "So Moses the servant of the LORD died there in the land of Moab, according to the word of the LORD. And he buried him in a valley in the land of Moab, over against Bethpeor: but no man knoweth of his sepulchre unto this day" (Deuteronomy 34:5-6). God Himself killed him and buried him and no man knows his sepulchre. I believe God did not want them to know because they might have worshipped his grave or body or carried it with them. So God kept the tomb a secret. But the point is that this same Moses, whose body had been buried hundreds of years ago, reappeared and he was identifiable.

> And after six days Jesus taketh Peter, James, and John his brother, and bringeth them up into an high mountain apart, And was transfigured before them: and his face did shine as the sun, and his raiment was white as the light. And, behold, there appeared

unto them Moses and Elias talking with
him (Matthew 17:1-3).

Though his body was in the grave, he as a person was
alive and was recognized. The soul is you and it does not die
and it lives on after the body is dead. Another example is the
story of the rich man and Lazarus. The text reads,

> And it came to pass, that the beggar
> died, and was carried by the angels into
> Abraham's bosom: the rich man also died,
> and was buried; And in hell he lift up his
> eyes, being in torments, and seeth Abraham
> afar off, and Lazarus in his bosom. And
> he cried and said, Father Abraham, have
> mercy on me, and send Lazarus, that he
> may dip the tip of his finger in water, and
> cool my tongue; for I am tormented in this
> flame (Luke 16:22-24).

There are three persons in this text who had all died. But
they were all alive although their bodies were in the grave.
The person, the soul, was alive. The rich man was tormented
in the flames. Lazarus was comforted, as well as Abraham.

There are many times in the scripture where people are
referred to as souls.. "And fear came upon every soul: and
many wonders and signs were done by the apostles" (Acts
2:43). Also, in Acts 3:23 we read, "And it shall come to pass, *that*
every soul, which will not hear that prophet, shall be destroyed
from among the people." Another reference says, "Let every
soul be subject unto the higher powers. For there is no power
but of God: the powers that be are ordained of God" (Romans
13:1). So we see again we as people can be called souls.

There are times when the word flesh is used to refer to the soul, and sometimes something different from the soul, according to scriptures. The following is an example, "*This I say then, Walk in the Spirit, and ye shall not fulfil the lust of the flesh. For the flesh lusteth against the Spirit, and the Spirit against the flesh: and these are contrary the one to the other: so that ye cannot do the things that ye would*" (Galatians 5:16-17).

Remember I noted before that there is nothing inherently sinful about the body. The body does what the inner being tells it to do. Jesus Christ Himself had a body like ours yet He was without sin. So when it says the flesh lusts, it is not referring to the physical body but the soul, you, the person that you are. The body cannot sin if it is not led by the soul. The soul is self-conscious, it only wants to please itself.

The natural man has a soul but he cannot receive the things of God because God communicates to us through our spirits. We read in 1 Corinthians 2:14; "But the natural man receiveth not the things of the Spirit of God: for they are foolishness unto him: neither can he know *them,* because they are spiritually discerned." God's words says that "no flesh should glory in His presence" (1 Corinthians 1:29). This is not talking about the body, but the self: lifting up ourselves, our achievements, instead of giving glory to God.

We must live lives where our souls will be subject to the will of God and not to our own wills. We have to live by the Word and Spirit of God, not just what we want but what He says.

At times the word flesh is used in reference to family relationship, as in Genesis 37:27. Sometimes it is used to refer to the physical body, like in Proverbs 5:11. There are instances when flesh is used to mean food, for example in Psalm 78:20, 27. It has also been used to refer to all living animals and man (Genesis 6:13, 17). It has been used as opposed to the Spirit as in Luke 24:39. Additionally the scripture speaks of living in the flesh to refer to earthly lifestyles (Philippians 1:22). In Isaiah 31:3, a distinction is also made between the weakness of the flesh and the power of the Spirit of God. And in Romans 7:14 flesh refers to the carnal nature.

We can know when we are walking in the flesh and not in the Spirit. Paul says there will be division, party spirit and the works of the flesh. So we can test ourselves to see whether we are soulish or we are living in the Spirit.

Now there are clear distinctions made between the soul and the spirit. I strongly reject the argument that the soul and the spirit are always used interchangeably when talking about the inner nature of man. Let us look at two scriptures that I believe will make it very clear that there are three distinct parts of man. We read from Hebrews 4:12, "For the word of God *is* quick, and powerful, and sharper than any two-edged sword, piercing even to the dividing asunder of soul and spirit, and of the joints and marrow, and *is* a discerner of the thoughts and intents of the heart."

The reference in Hebrews 4:12 talks about the power of the Word of God, and how sharp and precise it is. It says that the Word of God is so powerful that even though the soul and the spirit are so difficult to untangle, or so closely connected that man cannot divide it, but the Word of God can. The Word of God can also divide the joints and the marrow, no matter how closely connected they might be. It discerns the very thoughts and intents of the heart. Things that we cannot divide or reach or see, the Word of God can reach and divide them. Thus the argument that the soul and spirit here are symbolic is difficult to believe. They are two different entities in a man's life, soul and spirit, just as the other parallels made are distinct.

Jesus said that the most costly thing that a man possesses is his soul. He says, "For what shall it profit a man, if he shall gain the whole world, and lose his own soul? Or what shall a man give in exchange for his soul?" (Mark 8:36-37). The soul is the most costly thing that a man has. It is worth more than the whole world. Therefore we must make sure that it is secure in Jesus Christ. You must commit it to Him and obey Him so that your soul would never perish or be lost. How can it be lost? If it is not in the hand of God then it is lost. If it finds itself in Hell, it is lost and will suffer. Jesus says He has power to cast it to Hell.

In Apostle Paul's benediction in 1 Thessalonians 5:23, he states: "And the very God of peace sanctify you wholly; and *I pray God* your whole spirit and soul and body be preserved blameless unto the coming of our Lord Jesus Christ." He says that 'your whole spirit and soul and body be preserved blameless.' It means the entire man is to be blameless. And note, the entire you consists of body, soul and spirit.

In concluding this chapter, I want to speak briefly on the spirit. Briefly because many people don't have a problem understanding that they have a spirit; their main concern is the soul.

We receive things from God through our spirits. Paul says, "The Spirit itself beareth witness with our spirit, that we are the children of God" (Romans 8:16). So the Holy Spirit speaks to our spirit. As Jesus said in John 4:24, "God *is* a Spirit: and they that worship him must worship *him* in spirit and in truth." Proverbs 20:27 says, "The spirit of man *is* the candle of the LORD, searching all the inward parts of the belly." God lights our spirits so that we can see things. God has a light in us and that light is the spirit He has given to us. He shows us things through that light.

The Minirth Guide for Christian Counselors define

the spirit in this way: "The spirit is the supernatural part of man given by God at birth. It is not to be equated with the Holy Spirit of God received by Christians at the time of conversion."[7] God created us in such a way that we can communicate with Him through our spirit.

Let Us Talk About Death

"Death is a great mystery, perhaps the greatest mystery of human existence. As a mystery, death is problematic to humans."[8]

There is much that has been written about death. We see people dying every day, yet we don't fully understand death. According to the Bible there are different types of death.

There is physical death. It is the separation of soul and spirit from the body. James 2:26 says, "For as the body without the spirit is dead, so faith without works is dead also." So death is when the spirit leaves the body. The body without the spirit is dead. About Jesus, Mark writes, "And Jesus cried with a loud voice, and gave up the ghost" (Mark 15:37).

Then there is spiritual death; the separation of living man from God. For that person, although he is alive physically, he is separated from God because he does not obey God or does not believe and practice what God says. "But she that liveth in pleasure is dead while she liveth" (1 Timothy 5:6). And again Jesus said in Matthew 8:22, "But Jesus said unto him, Follow me; and let the dead bury their dead." The first 'dead' Jesus mentioned were not dead physically, but they were spiritually dead. Jesus called the unbelievers dead. The prodigal son's father said he was dead, but he was

---

[7]   Minirth, *The Minirth Guide for Christian Counselors*, 12

[8]   Grenz, *Theology for the Community of God*, 574

physically alive. Luke 15:24, "For this my son was dead, and is alive again; he was lost, and is found. And they began to be merry."

Eternal death is sometimes referred to as the second death. That means eternal separation from God. That is where you die without Christ as your Lord and Savior. That person is eternally lost; yet alive, but separated from God and everything good. That person will eventually be cast into the lake of fire, where there is no hope of salvation. Revelation 21:8 says, "But the fearful, and unbelieving, and the abominable, and murderers, and whoremongers, and sorcerers, and idolaters, and all liars, shall have their part in the lake which burneth with fire and brimstone: which is the second death."

From all these scriptures we realize that death is separation. One type of death is separation of spirit from body, which is also separation from life on earth. The body cannot live on earth without the spirit.

Then we have separation from fellowship with God. One is alive physically but has no relationship with God. And finally we have eternal separation from God. To die without God in one's life is to be separated from God for ever. That is the worst form of death; because with this form of death you end up in the lake of fire forever. It is called eternal damnation.

"The thing to be feared is not the first but the second death, not the parting of the soul from the body, but the final separation of the entire man from God. This is death indeed. This death kills all peace, joy, happiness, hope. When God is gone, all is gone."[9]

---

[9] C. H. Spurgeon, The Cheque *Book of the Bank of Faith*; (New York: Armstrong and Son, 1889), 115

In order for one to avoid eternal death he must put saving faith in the redemptive work of Jesus Christ for him, through His death and resurrection. However it must be done before physical death. You cannot change your decision after that death. As the writer of the book of Hebrews says, "And as it is appointed unto men once to die, but after this the judgment" (Hebrews 9:27).

Chapter 11

Morality And Immorality

"All societies must have a sense of moral order to survive. Without a differentiation between good and evil, relationships in human communities are impossible."[1]

Man is trying his best to be the standard for morality, without God. But sinful man can never be the standard for morality. Morality must come from someone who is moral himself; someone who is holy and only God is totally holy, and therefore has the right to set the standard for morality.

According to R. C. Sproul, "Humanness is defined by what human beings do. Hence, if the normal human being engages in premarital sexual intercourse, we conclude that such activity is normal and therefore 'good'."[2] Something does not become right or wrong based on the normative or what the majority is doing. In some parts of the world, there are more people living in common-law relationships than

---

[1] Paul G. Hiebert, R. Daniel Shaw and Tite Tienou, *Understanding Folk Religion* (Grand Rapids, Michigan: Baker Books, 1999), 197

[2] R. C. Sproul, *Following Christ* (Wheaton, Illinois: Tyndale House Publishers, Inc., 1983), 297

those who are married, but that does not make it morally right. So basically, the world is saying that our morality must come from what the majority says.

R. C. Sproul continues to expose the weakness of statistics based morality, (the morality that says because the majority is doing it therefore it is good). He cites the conveniences and inconveniences of this approach. He says, "This method achieves great popularity when applied to some issues but breaks down when applied to others. If we do a statistical analysis of the experience of cheating among students or lying among the general public, we discover that a majority of students have at some time cheated and that everyone has at some time lied."[3] So since all have lied at some time should lying be declared morally right because statistics shows one hundred percent have lied? Morality cannot come from popular opinion. It comes from what God has said.

Man sets up standards and laws based on what he believes or what he wants to practice. His belief affects his morality. If he wants to practice homosexuality for example, he seeks to pass a law that will allow him to practice this without legal consequences. If a man believes it is wrong to abuse animals, he will seek to pass a law to prevent people from abusing animals. Your belief affects your behavior and your behavior testifies to your belief. God has set the moral standard for us in scripture. It is we who have to change our behavior to line up with His moral standard.

There is a push for personal freedom from God. Man does not want God to tell him what to do. But we can never go away from God and not experience chaos. He alone knows all things and what's best. And since we were created

---

[3] Sproul, *Following Christ,* 297-298

in His image, within us is a built-in consciousness of right and wrong even though we try hard to ignore and deny it.

The people from the days of Noah did not want the knowledge of the Almighty. Their thoughts were evil continually. In the end they perished in the flood. Job 21:13-15 states, "They spend their days in wealth, and in a moment go down to the grave. Therefore they say unto God, Depart from us; for we desire not the knowledge of thy ways. What *is* the Almighty, that we should serve him? and what profit should we have, if we pray unto him?" Reading from the following chapter might help you understand that Job, that great man, was indeed referring to the people of Noah's days. Let us look at the language of those men in the days of Noah; "Hast thou marked the old way which wicked men have trodden? Which were cut down out of time, whose foundation was overflown with a flood: Which said unto God, Depart from us: and what can the Almighty do for them? Yet he filled their houses with good *things:* but the counsel of the wicked is far from me" (Job 22:15-18).

The same attitude that the people had then about God and morality is what is being manifested today. They do not want knowledge of the Almighty. They say to God 'depart from us; we will have it our way'. People have not learned from history. As a matter of fact persons prefer to tell themselves that the things the Bible speaks about are myths and untruths. But at the end the consequences will be terribly great for not obeying God. The added tragedy is that we will not be able to repent at that time. Let us believe and obey the Bible. By so doing we will have the right standards of morality.

To many, the problem is not whether there is right or wrong, good and evil, but who says what is right or wrong. It is not what the majority says but who is saying it. It is how powerful those who are speaking for a particular thing are, in order for it to be seen as good. R. C. Sproul says,

> We seek a way to find the right, which is neither subjective nor arbitrary. We seek norms and principles that transcend prejudice or mere societal conventions. ...Ultimately we seek a knowledge of the character of God, whose holiness is to be reflected and mirrored in our patterns of behavior. With God there is a definite and absolute black and white. The problem for us is to discover which things belong where.[4]

There are some areas that we may call 'gray areas'. But those gray moral areas are minimal and do not affect us much. It means that we can live without them. The things that are absolutely necessary for morality are absolutely clear. There may be things that one may not understand in the Bible. But the most important things are absolutely clear so that all can understand. They are not parables, symbols, types or any such but plain and simple language. For example, matters such as where we come from; how to be saved; is there life after death; what is sin; how to live here on earth in relation to God and our neighbours; these and many other things are very clear. No gray areas there. So sometimes the excuses people give are unreasonable.

We must start doing what we know is correct before we tackle what we are not so sure of. It is like some students sitting exams in school. They start by doing what they know and after that, if time permits, they try to deal with whatever

---

[4] Sproul, *Following Christ*, 301

they are not sure about. Before you can count a million dollars, you should know one dollar. If you don't know one, you will never be able to count a million. To get to a hundred you start with one. In everything one must learn the basic before he can master the whole.

Another lens through which we can look at morality is in terms of what people do for personal safety. People are very concerned about their protection, and so they take drastic steps to try to protect themselves. They are afraid of losing their jobs so they try to take action to prevent that. Sometimes they take steps to try to protect themselves from becoming victims. In general they try to protect themselves from the unseen. But what means do they use to protect themselves? For some persons, they use whatsoever they believe will offer them the protection that they need, even criminal and ungodly means. This is why belief matters very much in matters of morality and immorality.

In attempting to protect themselves and their practices or what they love, some people will actually practice evil. They go to the occultist or the witchcraft worker. They seek their ancestor spirit or the spirit of the dead. There are those who will seek other beings from the unseen world to talk to them and offer them guidance. At times those rituals take different forms; sometimes even human sacrifices. They are seeking protection and blessing by practicing evil. Paul G. Hiebert et al write, "People around the world seek hidden knowledge from gods, spirits, ancestors, and other beings, who are believed to know the unknown. The organic methods people used to obtain guidance vary greatly from culture to culture, but some common patterns emerge."[5]

Calling on those ancestor spirits or unseen spirits for

---

[5]   Hiebert et al, *Understanding Folk Religion,* 176

guidance or to speak to them is to actually call on demons. Thus they are really calling on Satan to protect them. Ironically they call on evil to protect them from evil. They are calling on Satan to protect them from Satan. One cannot fight evil with evil. Evil cannot protect you from evil. And what seems to be protection sometimes comes at a greater price than money. It is life, human life. And sometimes it is to introduce practices that are immoral in a nation, such as abortion.

Generally people know that there is evil around. Some say they don't believe in God because they have made covenant with the devil. Evil comes from the devil and those who follow him practice and promote evil, even though they might do it in secret, or do it believing that they are protecting themselves.

In my culture it is common that if you have a decent job, a business or anything valuable, you would be told to protect yourself, or as they would say, 'help yourself.' Some would even offer to take you to the places and persons where you would receive your protection, or 'guard'. At times people receive things to wear on the body or to place in their home or business place. Sometimes one even has to go through certain rituals. Prayers have been offered for persons, who after they went through those rituals became possessed and in need of deliverance.

Is it possible to determine right and wrong without God? Is there another way? There is a dangerous philosophy of morality now that says as long as it can bring in money it is good. All we have to do they say in their philosophy, is to repackage, re-label the same old practice. For example, we don't call people prostitutes anymore. That is degrading, insensitive and sounds immoral. We call them 'sex workers.' We don't call people homosexuals, as this brings bad memories. We call them 'gay', happy. They are trying to beautify gross sin, making sin look appealing. In addition they say these things will improve the economy.

There is very little concern about foundational values, the health of people and the nation and the general degradation of society. We are no longer concerned about the morality of the thing nor are we concerned about right and wrong. This kind of thinking says, as long as we can get money for it, let's do it. It is like what Walldo Beach says, "We have to rob Peter to pay Paul."[6]

With this kind of thinking we may not even be aware of what we are teaching. This kind of principle says whatsoever will bring us money, moral or immoral, it is good, as long as it brings in money. This unwise logic says we can rob a man, as long as it will bring us money, it is ok. One can bring cocaine into the country as long as it will bring in money and help the economy, it can be allowed. It does not matter how many social ills come with it, or how many health problems are created. We can practice money laundering or any other sinful practices as long as money is coming in. We don't care what people do to get the money. We don't care if the money is clean or not. As long as we can get it, that's fine. Something is wrong with this kind of morality; the morality that's teaches that the most important thing is to benefit economically.

Man is too selfish to be the standard for morality. Morality and standards for life must come from God. Human beings are too selfish, too bias, too partial, too human and too sinful to be the ones to set the standard for morality.

According to Norman Geisler,

---

[6] Waldo Beach, *Christian Ethics in the Protestant Tradition,* (Atlanta: John Knox Press, 1988), 47

The most significant root of the sexual revolution in the modern world is what Nietzche (d. 1900) called 'the death of God'. He said, 'God is dead and we have killed Him,' But when God dies, then all objective value dies with Him. As the Russian novelist Fyodor Dostoyevsky (d. 1881) observed in *The Brothers Karamazov*, when God dies, then anything is permitted. The truth is that when we kill the moral Lawgiver, then there is no basis left for the moral law.[7]

---

[7] Norman L. Geisler, *Christian Ethics: Contemporary Issues &Options*, (Grand Rapids, Michigan: Baker Academic, 2010), 261

Chapter 12

Sexual Evilution

Yes, 'evilution' is my play on the word evolution. The purveyors of sexual sin and immorality contend that we are evolving into greater awareness, freedom and truth. But it is clear, even to honest observers that their path is leading not to a healthy utopia but a destructive dystopia.

The first institution that was created was marriage. It was created within the six days of the creation of the world by God Himself. As a matter of fact the first one to perform a marriage ceremony was God Himself. He was the Father-giver and the witness. I believe He also delivered the first sermon on marriage, and the sermon title was, 'It is Not Good for Man to be Alone'.

Before there was school, before there was church or any other institution, God instituted marriage. This must be very important to Him as well as to us. In order for us to have a good nation we must have good families. One of the major reasons that our prisons are filled with young men is because the young men are raised up without one or both parents in their lives. There is a breakdown in the family. People are not having children as God intended; not in the bounds of marriage and proper family life. Persons are having sex without commitment to proper family life. Instead they are having sex outside of marriage and promoting sexual immorality.

Now there is sex that might take place within the bounds of marriage (between husband and wife) that is immoral. For example, when a husband rapes his wife or when there is anal sex. Even though it is done between husband and wife, it is immoral.

Let us look deeper at some sexual practices that God calls immoral.

Adultery

Adultery is sexual relations by married people outside of their marriage bonds. It is married people having sex with people other than their spouses. But Jesus took it one step further. He said it is sin when a married person looks on someone who is not his spouse and imagines sex with the individual in his heart. "But I say unto you, That whosoever looketh on a woman to lust after her hath committed adultery with her already in his heart" (Matthew 5:28).

"Typical of the prevailing secular view of sex is that whatever is done between consenting adults is okay. The Bible, on the other hand, condemns adultery, fornication, homosexuality, and other forms of sexual perversion."[1] Adultery is condemned both in the Old and New Testaments. One of the Ten Commandments says, "Thou shalt not commit adultery" (Exodus 20:14).

But it wasn't just the law or a commandment to the Jews only. It was to the rest of the world as well. The Bible says to

---

[1] Geisler, *Christian Ethics,* 260

all, "And he saith unto them, Whosoever shall put away his wife, and marry another, committeth adultery against her. And if a woman shall put away her husband, and be married to another, she committeth adultery" (Mark 10:11-12).

The punishment for adultery in the Old Testament was harsh. The person was to face the death penalty, as we read in Leviticus 20:10; "And the man that committeth adultery with *another* man's wife, *even he* that committeth adultery with his neighbour's wife, the adulterer and the adulteress shall surely be put to death." That death was cruel and sharp. It was death by stoning. "They say unto him, Master, this woman was taken in adultery, in the very act. Now Moses in the law commanded us, that such should be stoned: but what sayest thou?" (John 8:4-5). God saw the sin of adultery as a very grievous sin and tried to put measures in place so that His people would avoid it at all times.

But in the new covenant Jesus removed the death penalty, or should I say rather, it was not included in the new covenant. Nowhere in the New Testament did adultery carry the death penalty, although it remained a terrible sin.

Fornication

The definition for the word 'fornication' from the Theological Dictionary of the New Testament comes from "Porne (from pernemi, to sell) literally means 'harlot for hire' (Greek harlots were usually slaves)."[2] So when one is a fornicator he/she is a slave; a slave you hire. This is very degrading. Now we know many women are being sold for sex and this is one

---

[2] Geoffrey W. Bromiley, Gerhard Kittel, and Gerhard Friedrich, *Theological Dictionary of the New Testament,* (Grand Rapids, MI: Eerdmans 2006), 918-919

of the most heinous crimes there is. But the sad thing is that many have agreed to be sold as sex slaves.

There is another category of persons who commit fornication, not realizing that they are slaves to sex. "Pornos means 'whoremonger' then 'male prostitute'."[3] So it is not just referring to a female, but the man as well, as a sex slave. "The porneuo group is mostly used for the root znh and has such senses as 'to be unfaithful', 'to play the harlot'. It may be used of the prostitute or the betrothed or married woman who proves unfaithful."[4] Those who practice fornication are those who are unfaithful, unfaithful in their marriage, unfaithful to God Almighty.

"Porneia means 'fornication' (sometimes involving adultery); figuratively it is a term for apostasy as unfaithfulness to God."[5] So at times, that word can be used for both married and unmarried persons. But it is also used sometimes to refer to people who have abandoned their faith and gone away from God. Spiritually they have taken another husband. They have abandoned or left the Lord.

"Ekporneuo means 'to commit fornication'; to 'lean into fornication' and figuratively 'to turn aside from God and go after other gods'."[6] So figuratively, when you backslide, you have committed spiritual fornication. "Fornication involves paganism and defiles the individual, the family and the land."[7]

Thayer's definitions of 'porneuo' is "to prostitute one's body to the lust of another; to give one's self to unlawful

---

[3] Bromiley et al, *Theological Dictionary of the New Testament,* 918-919

[4] Bromiley et al, *Theological Dictionary of the New Testament,* 918-919

[5] Ibid

[6] Ibid

[7] Ibid

sexual intercourse, to commit fornication; metaphorically to be given to idolatry, to worship idols; to permit one's self to be drawn away by another into idolatry."[8]

Pornography comes from the same root word as fornication. Oxford Learner's Dictionary describes it as "Books, magazines, DVDs, etc. that describe or show naked people and sexual acts in order to make people feel sexually excited, especially in a way that many other people find offensive."[9] It also gives the time around when the word evolved: "Mid 19th cent.: from Greek *pornographos* 'writing about prostitutes', from *pornē* 'prostitute' + *graphein* 'write'."[10] So put together the two words say prostitute writings.

Richard Sauer and Linda Sauer, on March 29, 2007, posted the following: "The word pornography is composed of two Greek words. The first is porne, meaning harlot, which is akin to the word pernanai, meaning to sell. The second word is graphein, meaning to write. In other words pornography is literally the writing of harlots."[11] It is not just physical sex that is fornication. One can be fully involved in fornication online, on their phone, TV, etc even if they are not physically in touch with another human.

The Word of God had nothing good to say about fornication or people who commit it. The Bible says that

[8] J. H. Thayer, Thayer's Greek Definitions, (updated March 16, 2012) from e-sword Bible Study Software Program

[9] *Pornography*, Oxford Learner's Dictionaries, Accessed 2016 http://www.oxfordlearnersdictionaries.com/definition/english/pornography

[10] Oxford Learner's Dictionaries, *Pornography*

[11] Richard Sauer and Linda Sauer, *Pornography: A distortion of God's Plan, Answers in Genesis,* March 29, 2007. Accessed May 26, 2017. https://answersingenesis.org/morality/pornography-a-distortion-of-gods-plan

fornication is a sin against the body; it is also against Christ because we are members of Christ. "Know ye not that your bodies are the members of Christ? shall I then take the members of Christ, and make *them* the members of an harlot? God forbid." (1 Corinthians 6:15)

Fornicators have no place in heaven (Ephesians 5:3-6). It also says that the wrath of God comes on people who practice fornication and other forms of sin. Fornication is one of the sins that should not even be once mentioned among Christians (Ephesians 5:3). We are to flee from fornication (1 Corinthians 6:18). People who lived in fornication were excommunicated from the church (1 Corinthians 5:11-13).

Fornication was and is part of idol worship. Commenting on 1 Corinthians 6:19, Archibald Thomas Robertson says, "In Corinth was the temple of Aphrodite in which fornication was regarded as consecration instead of desecration. Prostitutes were there as priestesses of Aphrodite, to help men worship the goddess by fornication."[12]

Homosexuality

I have touched on this topic before but it merits further treatment because of the aggressive way it is being pushed today.

No one is born a homosexual or a lesbian. No, not one. Gay activists try to tell us that they are 'born that way'. "The cornerstone of the homosexual agenda is the myth that gays are born that way. They cannot help it. They are only living out who they really are. We can't solve the problem of same-sex marriages unless we address this falsehood that lies as a

---

[12] A.T. Robertson, *Word Pictures in the New Testament*, (Nashville: B&H Pub. Group, 2000)

root cause of their movement."[13] This is part of their agenda, to make people believe that they are born biologically different, that they are born with a homosexual gene.

> Recent media reports have led us to believe that science has indeed found a 'gay gene'. But a closer look reveals they've proven nothing of the sort. Family Research Council associates Peter Sprigg and Timothy Dailey, authors of Getting It Straight: What the Research Shows About Homosexuality, observe: 'The research shows no convincing evidence that anyone is 'born gay' and suggest that homosexuality results from a complex mix of developmental factors'.[14]

Human beings are all born the same way. All are born sinners with a sinful nature. Therefore we are all capable of committing the worst of sins. For example, children from a very tender age can lie, really well sometimes. It is as if they have the gift of lying. The truth is that everyone is born with a sinful nature and that makes it possible for all of us to be able to commit any type of sin. What then should be done? Should we legislate laws to allow these people to lie, because it seems they were born like that? What about those who have been stealing from very young. Should we say that he or she has a 'stealing gene' and therefore we should legislate laws to allow them to steal?

We all have sinful tendencies coming from an imperfect

---

[13] D. James Kennedy and Jerry Newcombe, *What's Wrong With Same-Sex Marriage?* (Wheaton, Illinois: Crossway Books, 2004), 97

[14] Kennedy and Newcombe, *What's Wrong With Same-Sex Marriage?* 97

soul. And so we all have to learn to discipline the areas of our lives that are wrong and want to control us. For some persons the weakness might not be a same-sex issue. It might be craving every beautiful woman who passes by. As soon as he sees them he wants to have sex with them, and if he cannot get them to consent, he may even rape them. What do we tell people struggling with these problems? Should excuses be made for them? Do they have a gene that is causing them to do this? No sir.

What then should a person do? We must realize that we have tendencies that are wrong inside of us and we must deal with them by mortifying them. Don't feed them. What you feed will most likely grow to be strong. Discipline this passion. We must recognize a thing as wrong and vow not to do that which is wrong. We should probably read about the dangers of such practices or lifestyles on not just ourselves, but on our family and nation as well. We should look to those who might be able to help or lead us to where we can find help. Seek a good professional counselor who might be able to help you. Abstain from individuals or groups which encourage you to continue in the old lifestyle.

People must acknowledge that the homosexual and lesbian and whole LGBTQ lifestyle is sin, and if it is sin, then it is wrong. This is despite the new theology of churches that cowardly bow to the threats and entreaties of the gay agenda. And if morally wrong they should not expect nations to pass laws to accept this lifestyle and practice. This is not about colour and race, it is about morality. For example, if stealing is wrong as we know it is, why should I lobby government to pass a law to allow stealing just because I have the passion and ability to steal? This law would be wrong and foolish.

You say what about tolerance? There are things that we

just can't tolerate. Should we be tolerating evil such as murder and rape? Jesus warned about the danger of tolerating that which is wrong. There are many scriptures against accepting evil, but we look at just one in Revelation 2:18-20.

> And unto the angel of the church in Thyatira write; These things saith the Son of God, who hath his eyes like unto a flame of fire, and his feet *are* like fine brass; I know thy works, and charity, and service, and faith, and thy patience, and thy works; and the last *to be* more than the first. Notwithstanding I have a few things against thee, because thou sufferest that woman Jezebel, which calleth herself a prophetess, to teach and to seduce my servants to commit fornication, and to eat things sacrificed unto idols.

Jesus said, I am against you because you have tolerated or allowed a false prophet to teach and seduce my people. I am against you.

Can we tolerate people who are taking crack cocaine, even if persons say they love it, that they are adults and will take it in the privacy of their bedrooms? Yes, people have the freedom of choice but at times because they might damage themselves and society, we have to pass laws that will curtail that freedom. There are times when we have to pass laws to protect people from themselves. Having the ability to do something does not necessarily make it the right thing to do.

'Same-sex marriage' is not a marriage. It is counterfeit. A counterfeit marriage is illegal and wrong and immoral. The one who defined what marriage is, and performed the first wedding, never defined it as same-sex. It was a male and female. The Bible said God made them male and female and everything outside of that is counterfeit. Same-sex marriage is like counterfeit money. It is not really money yet the conman is trying to force or trick people to accept it as real money. And such persons go further, asking governments to stamp it as legal, when they know it is not.

God created a marriage that is made up of a male and female; not male with male and female with female. Kennedy and Newcombe put it beautifully;

> If you have a light bulb out and you call the maintenance man to fix it, he doesn't bring over a new fixture as if to somehow attach one fixture to the other. Nor do we try to attach one light bulb to another. Instead, they attach a bulb (sometimes called male) to the fixture (sometimes called female). Similarly, we don't try and take an electric plug (sometimes called a male) and try and attach it into another plug (another male). They don't fit. Instead, the plug fits into an outlet (sometimes called a female). In short, homosexuality is against nature.[15]

So in short this is a counterfeit marriage. No children can come out of this union, because it takes a male and a female to produce children. And, one of the reasons for the union of marriage is procreation. A man cannot naturally

---

[15] Kennedy and Newcombe, *What's Wrong With Same-Sex Marriage?* 54-55

get impregnated by another man and carry a baby for nine months. It cannot pass the test of true marriage.

Maybe we need to look at some of the things that the proponents of same-sex unions are not telling us about this lifestyle. They want to force their teaching on society and brain-wash us. All of a sudden they have become family-life teachers. They want to hold seminars everywhere and they want to be able to teach children at school. But what do they teach?

> A Catholic student at Cornell University desired to serve as an RA (resident assistant). However, he had no idea what the training would entail. He and other trainees were forced to watch hours of xxx-rated pornographic homoerotic films, while being observed by a professor. If they showed any sign of disgust or revulsion, they were forced to watch more film or they failed the orientation. This sounds more like the Chinese reeducation camps than a broad-minded university education.[16]

What they are doing is brain-washing people; forcing people to accept something against their will. It's like they try to isolate you to convince you that everyone else is fine with it, therefore there must be something wrong with you.

They want to teach our children from early that this lifestyle is normal. They want to literally force it down your throat. "Same-sex marriage is using the force of law

---

[16] Ibid 27

to persuade others to accept the unacceptable."[17] In other words they will go all the way to push their beliefs on others, and so they spend a lot of money to see that their agenda is passed and accepted.

Kennedy and Newcombe continue;

> The legalization of marriage is so important to homosexuals because in their minds legal means moral. We live in a society where God and His standards have been removed. If you do not go to God's word for the standards of right or wrong, good or evil, where do you go? To the law; you go to the law for all standards. So if the law says it's legal. Then you are ok.[18]

But friends, the law may make something legal, but it doesn't make it right or wrong. God is the only and final arbiter of what is right or wrong. The book, What's Wrong with Same-Sex Marriage, addresses the topic in depth, and I would like to reiterate some of their points and comment on others. The first reason Kennedy and Newcombe oppose homosexuality is because according to them, "God opposes homosexuality."[19] They cited that the Bible condemns it and so do they.

The second reason for their opposition is, "Same-sex marriage (and same-sex conjugal relations) goes against the natural order. Male with male and female with female just does not work physically."[20]

---

[17] Kennedy and Newcombe, *What's Wrong With Same-Sex Marriage?* 28

[18] Ibid, 32

[19] Ibid, 53

[20] Ibid, 54

> It goes against all of recorded history. We
> are looking at about five thousand years of
> recorded history with marriage being one
> man and one woman together for their
> mutual enjoyment and the protection of
> their children. Yes, there was homosexuality
> in antiquity, and there has been polygamy
> in several places in the world, and it is
> still practiced among Muslims and tribal
> people (and some Mormons). The norm
> has been marriage between two people
> of the opposite sex. Homosexuality has
> in virtually all societies been viewed as a
> perversion and not normal.[21]

Even though it has been in society for thousands of years,
society has never accepted homosexuality as something good.
Most nations barely tolerated it. And the Bible is very clear
that God has destroyed nations for their homosexual lifestyle.
Such is recorded in Genesis chapter 19 and Romans chapter 1.

Another reason cited by Kennedy and Newcombe is, "It
will hurt children. When Rosie O'Donnell's six-year-old son
asked, 'Mommy, why can't I have a daddy?' he was pleading
not just for what he wanted, but for what he needed as well.
Rosie's answer, 'Because I'm the kind of mommy who wants
another mommy' illustrates the adult selfishness that drives
the same-sex marriage movement."[22]

You may be wondering who is Rosie O'Donnell. She is an
American comedian, actress, author, television personality

---

[21] Kennedy and Newcombe, *What's Wrong With Same-Sex
Marriage?* 56

[22] Ibid, 57

and a lesbian rights activist. Most likely you might have seen her on the TV show, 'The View' or her own show, 'The Rosie O'Donnell Show.' She and people like her don't care much about who their lifestyles affect; adult, child, relatives, friends, state, law and order. They are just out to have their own way. And in the meantime individuals and societies are being destroyed.

Kennedy and Newcombe continue; "It will sink the culture from civilization to barbarianism – a major step. Craig Parshall point out, 'There's never been a society ever in the history of the world that has ever survived this kind of perversion.'"[23] They cited ancient Rome and the Soviet Union as examples of those that went down because of that lifestyle.

Another reason they gave against same-sex unions is, "It destabilizes all of society."[24] The scripture says it plainly in Psalm 11:3, "If the foundation be destroyed, what can the righteous do?" If there is not the proper foundation of the traditional family then all other grounds are sinking sand.

This next reason is very important. "It opens Pandora's box in the legalization of all sexual perversions. What next?"[25] If we are not careful very soon there will be laws allowing people to marry their pets or animals. And they will say 'this is my goat, and I can do what I want to in the privacy of my home with my goat'. Maybe the government would say the only law that would be passed is that the animal must not be consumed afterwards. Gross, isn't it? The point is where will it stop?

---

[23] Kennedy and Newcombe, *What's Wrong With Same-Sex Marriage?* 62-63

[24] Ibid, 63

[25] Ibid, 64

Kennedy and Newcombe give many more reasons why they oppose same-sex marriage but for the purpose of this book just one more reason will suffice. By the way, if only one of those reasons is true, then that alone is enough for us to reject same-sex marriage. "Same-sex marriages can produce no natural offspring."[26] What if fifty percent of this world was homosexual? What would become of the population of the world? How many people would we have with no children? Now, even China is allowing their people to have more children. Could you imagine if half of the population had none? Who would take care of the elderly population? What about the continuity of mankind? These are just some of the questions that need to be asked.

Let us look at their lifestyle a little bit. "Former Secretary of Education Bill Bennett, author of the Book of Virtues, contrasted tobacco use with promiscuous homosexuality: 'So what does smoking do to your life? Smoking takes six to seven years off your life. Very important, very serious; we should address that. Promiscuous male homosexuality takes maybe 20 to 30 years off your life."[27]

It shortens your life about thirty percent. Why should laws be passed for such destruction of life? The homosexuals, in their teaching about this lifestyle, don't tell the public these things. "The Centers for Disease Control in Atlanta have pointed out in interviews (through the interview process) that a typical active male homosexual might have two to three hundred partners a year."[28] About three hundred partners a year! The average is almost one a day.

---

[26] Ibid, 66
[27] Kennedy and Newcombe, *What's Wrong With Same-Sex Marriage?* 88
[28] Ibid, 88-89

The multiplicity of sex partners brings all kinds of diseases. The proponents of this lifestyle must tell people the truth.

There is a very high death rate among homosexuals because of the lifestyle. "Listen to what one ex-gay, who was about age thirty-five, told our television audience: 'At this point in my life, there have been at least 94 people that I know have died of AIDS, personal friends in the past three years."[29] In three years almost a hundred of his friends have died because of such a lifestyle. It is worse than gangs that are dealing with illegal substances. This lifestyle is dangerous to the very person who is practicing it. It is self-destructive.

> The Family Research Council has put together a very helpful book, drawing only from secular, widely accepted sources, such as the Centers for disease Control (CDC) of Atlanta. This book is called Getting it Straight, and was written by Peter Sprigg and Timothy Dailey. They point out that homosexuals in America still represent the greatest population with HIV infection.[30]

If they are the highest in America where all forms of protection are available in addition to education about how to practice safe sex, it just may be the highest in other nations as well.

Other sicknesses and STI's seem to multiply very quickly within this group. How? This group is involved in drug

---

[29] Ibid, 89

[30] Kennedy and Newcombe, *What's Wrong With Same-Sex Marriage?* 90

abuse and violence even in their sex acts, and the illnesses which many of them have is because of their lifestyles.

Some of them become possessed with evil spirits, as any gross sin can cause to happen. A number of them turn to the church for help in this regard. The advice to those who are not involved is never get involved, because it is difficult to get out, even when you want to leave. If you are involved, seek help to get out, no matter the cost. It is a dangerous lifestyle.

Bestiality

The BBC news of 28 November 2012, wrote,

> Animal welfare: Germany moves to ban bestiality. The German parliament's agriculture committee is considering making it an offense not only to hurt an animal but also to force it into unnatural sex. Offenders could face a hefty fine. A final vote will be held in Bundestag (lower house) on 14 December. Germany legalized bestiality (zoophilia) in 1969, except when the animal suffered 'significant harm'.[31]

It is called natural sex with animals. How can human beings have natural sex with animals? It is inhuman and unnatural. I also want you to note how long this law has been there, 1969. And nobody seemed bothered about it, not even the animal rights activists.

---

[31] Animal Welfare: Germany moves to ban bestiality. Published 28 November 2012. Accessed 2016. http://www.bbc.com/news/world-europe-20523950

The Holy Bible condemns human beings having sex with animals, and the penalty for such a practice in the Old Testament was death; death for the guilty person and the innocent animal (Leviticus 20:15-16). The Bible calls such practices confusion; confusion is madness. It says that these kinds of practices make individuals unclean and pollutes them, (Leviticus 18:23). It is not just the sex with animals, but also because beasts cannot consent. So the person involved is basically raping an animal. And who knows what kind of biological mix can happen between human and animal sex cells.

Rape and Incest

Rape is always violent. It is forcing someone into having sex. It goes beyond the momentary act to negatively affecting the individual's present and future life. A victim of rape has something taken from him/her that can never be replaced, even if the rapist is caught and punished. That victim has been 'damaged'.

No man is to rape any woman, no matter how beautiful she may look or how provocatively she may be dressed, or even if she is naked. This is not to promote nudity. The point is that there is no reason to rape. Her body is hers alone. Our body is the only property that God gave to us. This is the only property she dies with. She goes to the grave with it. Nobody should try to take it from her.

This is more than burglarizing a house, more than stealing from a bank, or robbing a church. In all of those, goods can be replaced. But when a rape has been committed, a life is being destroyed. Furthermore, divine property is being burgled and assaulted, for our bodies were given to us by God. It is the temple of God. The damage done to the person through rape cannot be quantified or fully seen or explained.

You can do without a lot of things in this world, but no one can live without his/her body. This shows how valuable the body is to us. Thus no one should steal any one's body. You may have nothing in this world but you have your body and no one should attempt to take it from you. But further to that, rape also assaults a person's soul leaving them battered emotionally and mentally.

Sometimes when a person is raped, they are blamed and shamed. But that should not be. Rape victims at times blame themselves for being raped, and they shouldn't either. For example, they tell themselves they were in the wrong place at the wrong time. They feel that they should have locked the door; they should have been with a group; they should have been more aware of their environment and so on. But this argument is neither good nor helpful. The victim is not to be blamed, nor should he/she blame him/herself. There are some fathers who rape their own children in their bedroom. Would you say that the child should not be in his/her room? And yes I have used the masculine pronoun because males both young and old can be raped as well.

The victim is not the problem. The rapist is the problem. There are some rape victims who feel that they are of no value and that is why they were raped or have been raped repeatedly. This is the reality in many incest cases. No, you are valuable. The rapist is the one who is contemptible and needs to be reported to the police and put behind bars.

With sexual practices outside of traditional marriage being promoted and even celebrated more and more, it is up to those of conscience and biblical faith to maintain and proclaim God's moral standards. We should not be ashamed for God's way leads to life and good for humanity. Neither should we be afraid to tell the truth even if it means having to stand against the latest fads in human 'evilution'.

Chapter 13

So-Called Irreconcilables
In The Bible

Bible bashers contend that the Bible is replete with inconsistencies and statements that are irreconcilable. In this chapter I will identify some of these and show how their objections are overblown and simply the futile attempts of theologically ignorant or lazy God haters.

Where Did Cain Get His Wife?

I am dealing with this question, not because of its importance to me, but because so many people ask it. I believe most of them know the answer but are asking merely to make a point. They want to bring up the topic of incest while others want to claim that there were people living on the earth before Adam and Eve. But the Bible makes no such reference, so the original question needs to be answered.

Some people say that the Bible says that Cain got his wife from the land of Nod, but the Bible does not say that. This is what the scriptures say; "And Cain went out from the presence of the LORD, and dwelt in the land of Nod, on the east of Eden. And Cain knew his wife; and she conceived, and bare Enoch: and he builded a city, and called the name of the city, after the name of his son, Enoch" (Genesis 4:16-17).

It is very possible that Cain took his wife before he went to Nod. The text says that he knew his wife and she conceived and bore Enoch. That knowing referred to in the text is sexually, as Adam 'knew' his wife and bear Cain and Abel. But Adam and Eve were married before they knew each other sexually and before they had sinned. So it is very possible that Cain moved to the land of Nod with his wife and they bore children there.

Cain went to the land of Nod which was uninhabited and settled there with his wife. They then built the city and called it after the name of his son.

Ken Ham, Andrew Snelling and Carl Wieland made some strong observations from the scriptures which would help us on our quest to answer the question of where Cain got his wife. Let us look at some of the points they made.

1. Adam was the first man (Genesis 2:7, 18-19 cf. 1Corinthinas 15:45).
2. Adam lived for 930 years (Genesis 5:5).
3. Eve was given that name because she was to be the mother of all living (Genesis 3:20).
4. Adam and Eve had many sons and daughters (Genesis 5:4).
5. Everything was very good when first created (Genesis 1:31).
6. This goodness was marred when 'By one man sin entered the world' (Romans 5:12, cf. Genesis 3).

7. The creation was cursed by God (Genesis 3:17, cf. Romans 8:20-22) because of Adam's sin.

8. Abraham was married to his half-sister (Genesis 20:12).

9. The laws of incest had their origin only at the time of Moses (Leviticus 18-20). Those nine basic points provide clues that suggest Cain must have married his sister.[1]

It is clear to me that Cain's wife was his sister. She was the child of Adam and Eve. God created Adam and Eve and told them to be fruitful and multiply. He spoke only to Adam and Eve. There were none before them and none other than them. And in a true sense we all came from them. The Bible says in Genesis 5:3-4, "And Adam lived an hundred and thirty years, and begat *a son* in his own likeness, after his image; and called his name Seth: And the days of Adam after he had begotten Seth were eight hundred years: and he begat sons and daughters." So inasmuch as the Bible did not mention Adam and Eve's daughters' names, it states clearly that they had both sons and daughters, after they had Cain and Seth.

This text in Genesis 4 does not give any one the right to say that there was another group of people apart from Adam and Eve's generation. But based on what we see in the scriptural text above, Adam and Eve had daughters.

I should state that it was not a sin then for one to marry his sister, because there was nobody else upon the earth to marry. Additionally, God had not given any command

---

[1] Ken Ham, Andrew Smelling, and Carl Wieland, *The Answers Book: Answers to the 12 Most-Asked Questions on Genesis and Creation/Evolution;* (Sunnybank, Australia: Creation Science Foundation Ltd., 1990), 115

then forbidding marrying their sisters. That law came long afterwards.

Cain married his own sister but it was not a sin. It is a sin now, and such an arrangement is no longer necessary. As a matter of fact the Bible says it is a great sin (Leviticus 18:6-10). There are many more chapters and books in the Bible that speak about the matter. But in the days of Cain, there was no choice. So I say again, Adam and Eve did not just have two sons, Cain and Abel. They had other children, including girls and that allows for the possibility of where Cain got his wife.

What Moses said and what Paul said differ

Another attempt to show error in the Bible is in regards to this: Numbers 25:9 says 24000 were killed. 1 Corinthians 10:8 says 23000 were killed when referring to the same event. What happened? Balaam was hired by Balak, King of Moab to curse the children of Israel. Instead of cursing them God supernaturally caused him to bless them. Balak was displeased with Balaam. But why could he not curse them? Because the people were living in covenant with God; therefore God protected them. But Balaam taught Balak a trick as to how to defeat the children of Israel; and that was to cause them to be involved in sin. Revelation 2:14 states it this way; "But I have a few things against thee, because thou hast there them that hold the doctrine of Balaam, who taught Balak to cast a stumblingblock before the children of Israel, to eat things sacrificed unto idols, and to commit fornication."

In other words, for God to remove His protection over them, they had to be living in sin. So Balaam advised Balak to have them enter into marriages with his people, the Moabites, and to commit sexual sins and to worship the gods of the Moabites, and God would have no choice but to turn His back on them. And that is exactly what happened, as recorded in Numbers 25. Because of those sins God killed 24000 of them, according to Numbers 25:9. God sent a plague, an epidemic among them because He was angry with them because of their sins.

So the total number recorded was 24000. But Paul, reporting or commenting on this same incident said in one day God killed 23000. Moses on the other hand had given the total figure. So there is no contradiction between Paul and Moses. And there is no problem in figures; one gave the total figure which was 24000 whereas the other referred to the worst day of the plague. Numbers 25:9 says, "And those that died in the plague were twenty and four thousand." 1 Corinthians 10:8 says on the same subject, "Neither let us commit fornication, as some of them committed, and fell in one day three and twenty thousand."

David's payment for the property he bought from Araunah

There seems to be a difference in the two accounts. 2 Samuel 24:24 says 50 shekels of silver was paid and 1 Chronicles 21:25 recorded 600 shekels as the price.

Before we go into the interpretation of the text, it is important to get the background of what caused this sacrifice, the buying of the sacrifice and the payment of the land. This all came about because David sinned against God by numbering the children of Israel against the will of God. As a matter of fact it seemed like a sin of pride. He wanted to show the size of his army. He seemed to express confidence in his army when it was God who had been his strength, and not his army.

The scripture puts it this way,

> And Satan stood up against Israel, and provoked David to number Israel. And David said to Joab and to the rulers of the people, Go, number Israel from Beersheba even to Dan; and bring the number of them to me, that I may know *it.* And Joab answered, The LORD make his people an hundred times so many more as they *be:* but, my lord the king, *are* they not all my lord's servants? why then doth my lord require this thing? why will he be a cause of trespass to Israel? Nevertheless the king's word prevailed against Joab. Wherefore Joab departed, and went throughout all Israel, and came to Jerusalem (1 Chronicles 21:1-4).

He wanted to know the strength of Israel for that would bring glory for him. The glory should have been to God and not the army or himself, because it was God who prepared them and gave them the victory. It was neither the might nor power of the army, but the fact that the Lord was with them.

Sadly, the very same people David had counted were being destroyed and killed by a plague sent by God. David then asked God to forgive him for his sin. Then God sent a prophet named Gad to offer David one of three choices of punishment. David had to choose.

> Either three years' famine; or three months to be destroyed before thy foes, while that

> the sword of thine enemies overtaketh *thee;*
> or else three days the sword of the LORD,
> even the pestilence, in the land, and the
> angel of the LORD destroying throughout
> all the coasts of Israel. Now therefore advise
> thyself what word I shall bring again to him
> that sent me. And David said unto Gad, I
> am in a great strait: let me fall now into
> the hand of the LORD; for very great *are*
> his mercies: but let me not fall into the
> hand of man. So the LORD sent pestilence
> upon Israel: and there fell of Israel seventy
> thousand men; (1Chronicles 21:12-14).

So David chose to fall into the hand of God for his punishment, to be disciplined. He said God was a merciful God, so he preferred to fall into God's hands. But God's discipline was very severe on David and Israel. God killed seventy thousand men and sent an angel into Jerusalem to destroy it.

When David saw the angel of the Lord standing with his sword drawn over Jerusalem, he fell on his face and begged for mercy. The Lord responded to him favourably; "Then the angel of the LORD commanded Gad to say to David, that David should go up, and set up an altar unto the LORD in the threshingfloor of Ornan the Jebusite" (1 Chronicles 21:18).

So this is how David ended up going to Ornan to buy the threshingfloor and the animals for the sacrifice. The following verse here in 1 Chronicles 21:20 is very important; "And Ornan turned back, and saw the angel; and his four sons with him hid themselves. Now Ornan was threshing wheat." No wonder Ornan wanted to give David the animals and the place for the sacrifice at no cost; free of charge. He and his sons had seen the angel and were afraid. So they were willing to do anything to stop the judgment of God.

So Ornan sold the land and the animals to David willingly, after David told him that he could not take it for free. He said it is a sacrifice to the Lord and a sacrifice must not be free of cost. It must be paid for. So David paid him for the place and the sacrifice.

Now the issue is that the amount he paid differs in the parallel accounts of the story. So we need to look at both texts closely and we will find the answer. 1 Chronicles 21:25 says, "So David gave to Ornan for the place six hundred shekels of gold by weight." The cross reference in 2 Samuel 24:24 says, " And the king said unto Araunah, Nay; but I will surely buy *it* of thee at a price: neither will I offer burnt offerings unto the LORD my God of that which doth cost me nothing. So David bought the threshingfloor and the oxen for fifty shekels of silver."

Now one of the passages says six hundred shekels of gold by weight, for the place. But this was for the entire land. Here is what Jamieson, Fausset and Brown say on the matter. "The sum mentioned here, namely fifty shekels of silver, about $50, was paid for the floor, oxen and wood instruments only, whereas the large sum in 1 Ch 21:25 was paid afterwards for the whole hill, on which David made preparations for building the temple."[2]

So the fifty shekels referred to in 2 Samuel was just for the threshingfloor and the oxen, whereas the rest of the money stated in 1 Chronicles 21:25 was for all that David bought from Ornan.

---

[2] A. R. Fausset, David Brown, and Robert Jamieson, *Jamieson, Fausset & Brown's commentary on the whole Bible* (Grand Rapids, MI: Zondervan Pub. House, 1961).

We must also observe from the text that one says six hundred shekels of gold and the other says fifty shekels of silver. So there are two different currencies used, gold and silver. Therefore the amount will be different based on which was more valuable at the time. So to use this text to say that there is contradiction in the Bible is not fair.

The mustard seed; Matthew 13:32

Jesus said it is the smallest seed; did Jesus lie?

What we have to do is to state exactly what Jesus said about the mustard seed. And the only way is to go to the text. It is found in three different places in the gospels, therefore we will look at all three references.

Matthew 13:31-32 says, "Another parable put he forth unto them, saying, The kingdom of heaven is like to a grain of mustard seed, which a man took, and sowed in his field: Which indeed is the least of all seeds: but when it is grown, it is the greatest among herbs, and becometh a tree, so that the birds of the air come and lodge in the branches thereof."

The book of Mark is the next reference and it reads in Mark 4:31-32, "*It is* like a grain of mustard seed, which, when it is sown in the earth, is less than all the seeds that be in the earth: But when it is sown, it groweth up, and becometh greater than all herbs, and shooteth out great branches; so that the fowls of the air may lodge under the shadow of it."

The last text is found in the book of Luke 13:19 and it states, "It is like a grain of mustard seed, which a man took, and cast into his garden; and it grew, and waxed a great tree; and the fowls of the air lodged in the branches of it."

None of those scriptures used the word smallest. So the case is closed. But for some it may not be satisfactory, so let us go deeper. The Apostle Paul called himself the least of the apostles. Was he the smallest? I don't think so. I think he was saying that as far as human worth is concerned 'I am nothing much'. Yet, God used him greatly, maybe more than any of the other apostles. I believe Jesus was saying this seed looks like nothing, but when it is sown in the field and it grows, you will see its true potential. And of course he was talking about the Kingdom of Heaven.

But even if we allow for the physical dimension of the seed, we must read it in context of who Jesus was speaking to. The Bible Knowledge Commentary says, "This seed was in fact the smallest of the garden seeds known. (Orchard seeds, though smaller, were unknown in that part of the world.) Also small as a mustard seed was a proverb by which people referred to something unusually small."[3]

Remember He was speaking a parable and to people living in Israel. He was using what they know to make His point about the Kingdom of Heaven, and telling them that no matter how small it looks now, it will grow. Furthermore, we must not despise small beginnings. Just as this small seed grows when it is sown, in like manner the Kingdom of Heaven will grow. He could not use a seed that they were not familiar with to teach them a lesson He expected them to understand.

Furthermore, least can signify insignificance, not always size. You can have a lesser number of currency notes in your pocket than another person does, but yours might be of more value. Jesus was talking about the importance of sowing that seed. If it is not sown it will remain only

---

[3] The Bible Knowledge Commentary on Matthew; An exposition of the Scriptures by Dallas Seminary Faculty; Editors, John F. Walvoord and Ray B. Zuck (Victory Books, 1983) 51

a very small seed, but if it is sown, its potential is huge. I am the least of my mother's children when it comes to education; but I am the first in terms of birth. Not the last, but the least.

Can God be using Israel as that mustard seed that will become a great tree that will shoot branches from every place? He used them as the beginning of the church. Did He not start with twelve apostles? Has it not spread through the entire earth because it was sown by Jesus Himself, when it was nothing in the eyes of the world?

The Word of God says in Deuteronomy 10:22, "Thy fathers went down into Egypt with threescore and ten persons; and now the LORD thy God hath made thee as the stars of heaven for multitude." And again in Isaiah 51:2 we read, "Look unto Abraham your father, and unto Sarah *that* bare you: for I called him alone, and blessed him, and increased him." God called Israel when they were nobody and made them great; and the church really came out of Israel because Jesus by physical birth was a Jew.

The Blind Men At Jericho

Matthew 20:29-34, Mark 10:46-52 and Luke 18:35-43 mention the healing of blind men by Jesus. These accounts contain different details, which some use to claim that there are errors in the Bible.

The text in Matthew says there were two blind men sitting by the wayside. It goes on further to say that Jesus touched their eyes and immediately their eyes received sight.

The text in Mark says clearly it was one blind man. It also gave his name and his father's name. In Luke we read that it was one blind man. So Mark and Luke are parallel texts, but not Matthew. Is there a problem? No.

Why should we assume that these three portions of scripture are referring to the same encounter? Is it just because all three happened in Jericho? Was it only once that Jesus went to Jericho?

The scriptures show us at least two separate incidents. One time He healed a man named Bartimaeus as Mark and Luke reported. Luke did not mention his name, but said clearly that it was one man. Matthew was reporting about a separate incident where Jesus healed two blind men.

Ryrie has this to say about the different accounts; "As to the number of blind men, if Mark and Luke said only one blind man then there would be an error, but if Bartimaeus was the more forward of the two, then it would be natural for one writer to focus on him while another might mention both of them."[4] Ryrie went on to say, "One is that the men pleaded with the Lord as he entered Jericho, but were not healed until he was leaving. The other is that since there were two Jerichos (old Jericho and the new city) the healing could have taken place after the group left old Jericho and as they were nearing the new Jericho."[5] But I would ask, why couldn't it be that one took place in the new Jericho and the other took place in the old Jericho?

So these are different accounts; one with one man and the other with two men. Any how we look at it there is no contradiction at all. We should search the scriptures for truth instead of searching for faults.

---

[4] Charles Caldwell Ryrie; *Basic Theology: A Popular Systematic Guide to Understanding Biblical Truth* (Chicago, IL: Moody Press, 1999), 114-115

[5] Ryrie, *Basic Theology*, 114-115

Problem with Mark 1:1-3; was Mark quoting Isaiah or Malachi?

Let us start with the scripture. "The beginning of the gospel of Jesus Christ, the Son of God; As it is written in the prophets, Behold, I send my messenger before thy face, which shall prepare thy way before thee. The voice of one crying in the wilderness, Prepare ye the way of the Lord, make his paths straight."

The writer said 'as it is written in the prophets'; he use the word 'prophets', plural. So he was quoting more than one prophet. Both Isaiah and Malachi spoke of the same prophecy that was referred to in Mark, thus the use of 'prophets'. Isaiah 40:3 reads, "The voice of him that crieth in the wilderness, Prepare ye the way of the LORD, make straight in the desert a highway for our God." In Malachi 3:1 we read, "Behold, I will send my messenger, and he shall prepare the way before me: and the Lord, whom ye seek, shall suddenly come to his temple, even the messenger of the covenant, whom ye delight in: behold, he shall come, saith the LORD of hosts."

In both Isaiah 40:3 and Malachi 3:1, the prophets were talking about John the Baptist coming before Christ to prepare the way for Him, the Messiah. Instead of criticizing this portion of scripture we should look at it and see the power of the Word of God. Isaiah lived about three hundred years before Malachi and prophesied that John the Baptist would come before Jesus; he would be the one to introduce Jesus Christ. Malachi prophesied the same thing and four hundred years later all was fulfilled. This can be nothing but the power of God.

What was the name of the priest present when David ate the showbread?

Mark 2:26, in referring to David eating the tabernacle bread, says Abiathar was the high priest at the time. The Old Testament record in 1 Samuel 21:1-6 states that it was Ahimelech was. What is the problem?

Let us turn to the texts in Mark 2:26 and the Old Testament text of 1 Samuel 21:1-6. Mark 2:26, "How he went into the house of God in the days of Abiathar the high priest, and did eat the shewbread, which is not lawful to eat but for the priests, and gave also to them which were with him?" 1 Samuel 21:1-6 tells us,

> Then came David to Nob to Ahimelech the priest: and Ahimelech was afraid at the meeting of David, and said unto him, Why *art* thou alone, and no man with thee? And David said unto Ahimelech the priest, The king hath commanded me a business, and hath said unto me, Let no man know any thing of the business whereabout I send thee, and what I have commanded thee: and I have appointed *my* servants to such and such a place. Now therefore what is under thine hand? give *me* five *loaves of* bread in mine hand, or what there is present. And the priest answered David, and said, *There is* no common bread under mine hand, but there is hallowed bread; if the young men have kept themselves at least from women. And David answered the priest, and said

unto him, Of a truth women *have been* kept from us about these three days, since I came out, and the vessels of the young men are holy, and *the bread is* in a manner common, yea, though it were sanctified this day in the vessel. So the priest gave him hallowed *bread:* for there was no bread there but the shewbread, that was taken from before the LORD, to put hot bread in the day when it was taken away.

The text in Mark did not say that Abiathar was the high priest who gave David the showbread, nor does it say that he was the high priest then. It says, 'In the days of Abiathar the high priest'. In other words, Abiathar was alive when that incident took place. But that does not necessarily mean he was the priest who gave David the bread, although he was alive. And I believe he may have been present when it happened but it could have been Ahimelech, the son of Abiathar, who handed the bread to David; but with the approval of his father.

Maybe the passage in 1 Chronicles 18:16 will shed some light on that. "And Zadok the son of Ahitub, and Abimelech the son of Abiathar, *were* the priests; and Shavsha was scribe". The point is that both Abiathar and Ahimelech were there when it happened. And King Saul slew the priest for their action because he thought that the priests were supporting David against him.

Now the scripture seems to suggest that both father and son had the same name or both of them were called Ahimelech and Abiathar. Let us look at some of these passages. 1 Samuel 23:6; "And it came to pass, when Abiathar the son of Ahimelech fled to David to Keilah, *that* he came down *with* an ephod in his hand." It says that Abiathar was the son of Ahimelech. However in 2 Samuel 8:17 says that Ahimelech was the son of Abiathar. Furthermore as 1 Chronicles 18:16 implies, they were both there when the incident took place. So if one says that the incident was in the days of Ahimelech or in the days of Abiathar, he/she wouldn't be wrong because they were both there when it happened.

The death of Judas

Acts 1:18 records Judas' death as he falling headlong and he burst open and all his bowels gushed out. Matthew 27:5 says Judas hanged himself. Some state that this is an obvious problem.

As before, let us look at the passages. Firstly Acts 1:18, "Now this man purchased a field with the reward of iniquity; and falling headlong, he burst asunder in the midst, and all his bowels gushed out." Matthew 27:5 reads, "And he cast down the pieces of silver in the temple, and departed, and went and hanged himself."

To me, we don't have a problem here. Matthew tells us that he committed suicide; he hanged himself. Peter went on in Acts and described how he died. So he said he fell and 'all his bowels gushed out.' So whether he fell on some stones or not, it is conceivable that he hanged himself but the rope or the branch broke and he fell on his stomach, perhaps on stones and his bowels gushed out. So in short Peter gave us more information about the death of Judas.

Remember as well that Luke is the author of the book of Acts, and he is a medical doctor. So he is giving us details as only a doctor can.

The different accounts of the time that Israel stayed in Egypt

Acts 7:6 says 400 years. Exodus 12:40 says 430 years.

Here is what Acts 7:6 says; "And God spake on this wise, That his seed should sojourn in a strange land; and that they should bring them into bondage, and entreat *them* evil four hundred years." And Exodus 12:40 says, "Now the sojourning of the children of Israel, who dwelt in Egypt, *was* four hundred and thirty years."

There are two accounts of the sojourning of Israel. The first one commences from the time God gave the promise to Abraham. And for this both Exodus 12:40 and Galatians 3:17 highlight 430 years. And, according to the Companion Bible Commentary, "The other starting from the recognition of his seed (Isaac), Genesis 21:12, also Acts 7:6 and Genesis 15:13, 400 years."[6]

So one is looking from the year God made the promise to Abraham which was 30 years before Isaac the seed came. So taken from Isaac it would be 400 years, but if taken from the time it was said to Abraham then it would be 430 years. So it is a matter of the point from which the writers took the story.

Adam Clarke, in his commentary on Acts 7:6 writes, "Moses says in Exodus 12:40 that the sojourning of the children of Israel in Egypt was 430 years. St. Paul has the same number in Galatians 3:17, and so has Josephus Ant.lib ii.cap1 sect. 9 in Bell.lib.v.cap.p, sect 4. St. Stephen used the round number of 400, leaving out the odd tens, a thing very common, not only in the sacred writers, but in

---

[6]   E. W. Bullinger, *The Companion Bible Condensed; Commentary on Exodus 12:40*, (Kregel Publication, 1995)

all others, those alone excepted who wrote professedly on chronological matters."[7]

Again let me say this is not referring only to the time when Joseph and his brethren went down to Egypt; that would be just about 215 years. So it is talking about from the time God made the covenant with Abraham. Adam Clarke gives us a proper division of the time. "For from Abraham's entry into Canaan to the birth of Isaac was 25 years, Gen 12:4, 17:1-21; Isaac was 60 years old at the birth of Jacob, Gen 25:26; and Jacob was 130 at his going down into Egypt, Gen 47:9; which three sums make 215 years. And then Jacob and his children having continued in Egypt 215 years more, the whole sum of 430 years is regularly completed."[8]

So it may be that Stephen started his count from the birth of Isaac while the others took it from the time the covenant was made with Abraham, thus giving us 30 years difference; or it might have been that Stephen just used the round number.

The age of Ahaziah

Two and twenty years old was Ahaziah when he began to reign, says 2 Kings 8:26.

Yet 2 Chronicles 22:2 says forty and two years old was Ahaziah when he began to reign.

What is happening here?

2 Kings 8:26 reads, "Two and twenty years old *was* Ahaziah when he began to reign; and he reigned one year

---

[7] Adam Clarke, *Adam Clarke's Commentary Practical and Explanatory on the Whole Bible,* (Grand Rapids, MI: Baker Book House, 1967)

[8] Clarke, *Adam Clarke Commentary on the Bible*

in Jerusalem. And his mother's name *was* Athaliah, the daughter of Omri king of Israel." The text in 2 Chronicles 22:2 says, "Forty and two years old *was* Ahaziah when he began to reign, and he reigned one year in Jerusalem. His mother's name also *was* Athaliah the daughter of Omri." So this looks like there were two Ahaziahs.

A similar issue appears when we look at the name Joram. It seems like there were two different Jorams. One was the son of Ahab in 2 Kings 8:25. The same verse says in the twelfth year of Joram, the son of Ahab King of Israel, did Ahaziah, the son of 'Jehoram' King of Judah begin to reign. He was 22 years old and he reigned one year. He was the son-in-law of the house of Ahab. And he went with Joram, the son of Ahab to war against Hazael King of Syria. He went with Joram in 2 Kings 8:28, but verse 24 of the same chapter says that Joram slept with his fathers and Ahaziah his son reigned in his stead.

But verse 29 is saying that Ahaziah, the son of Jehoram King of Judah went down to see Joram the son of Ahab in Jezreel because he was sick. So 2 Kings 8:29 introduced another Ahaziah; the Ahaziah of 2 Chronicles 22:2.

Did Omri have two daughters called Athaliah? The text in 2 Chronicles 22:2 says his mother's name 'also' was Athaliah, the daughter of Omri. Or, is this not saying that Athaliah had two sons with the same name, Azariah? So the scripture put the 'also' in there for us to note that she had two sons of the same name. We have already noted that there were two Ahaziahs. One began to reign at the age of 22 (2 Kings 8:26) and the other began to reign at 42; they were of the same mother, but not the same father.

There was an Ahaziah that was his biological son. This one was 22 years old when he began to reign (2 Kings 8:25). But the Ahaziah in 2 Chronicles 22:2 was not his biological son and not the same person, not the same age but the same mother; same mother but different fathers (2 Kings 8:26).

Jehoram is the father of the younger Ahaziah (2 Chronicles 22:1). So they made his youngest son king because all the others were slain (2 Chronicles 22:1). Remember Jehoram the king was 40 years old when he died (2 Chronicles 21:20). So Ahaziah as youngest son, could not be 42 years old at the time of his father's death.

So 2 Chronicles 22:2 is introducing another Ahaziah who was not the king's son and he started reigning at the age of 42. 2 Chronicles 22:5 says he went with Jehoram the son of Ahab King of Israel to war against Hazael King of Syria at Ramoth-Gilead. It did not say he went with his father, Jehoram.

2 Chronicles 22:6 goes back to the other Azariah the son of Jehoram, who went down to see Jehoram the son of Ahab at Jezreel because he was sick. When he came, he went out with Jehoram against Jehu. 2 Chronicles 22:9 says that Jehu sought Ahaziah and when he was caught, he was brought to Jehu. And when they had slain him, they buried him because, according to them, he was the son of Jehoshaphat, who sought the Lord; not the son of Jehoram.

How was the son of Jehoram killed? According to 2 Kings 9:27, "But when Ahaziah the king of Judah saw *this,* he fled by the way of the garden house. And Jehu followed after him, and said, Smite him also in the chariot. *And they did so* at the going up to Gur, which *is* by Ibleam. And he fled to Megiddo, and died there."

This chapter is saying that after he was hit he fled to Megiddo and died there. But of the other Ahaziah 2 Chronicles 22:9 says, "And he sought Ahaziah: and they caught him, (for he was hid in Samaria,) and brought him to Jehu: and when they had slain him, they buried him:

Because, said they, he *is* the son of Jehoshaphat, who sought the LORD with all his heart. So the house of Ahaziah had no power to keep still the kingdom." So Jehu killed both of them, but in two different ways and in two different places.

So these were two different Ahaziahs who were different in age. So there is no problem with that text, although I must confess, that it is a difficult text to unravel.

The beginning of Jehoiachin's reign

Two different texts commenting on the same king give a different age as to when he began to reign; (2 Kings 24:8 and 2 Chronicles 36:9). Is this a mistake?

"Jehoiachin *was* eighteen years old when he began to reign, and he reigned in Jerusalem three months. And his mother's name *was* Nehushta, the daughter of Elnathan of Jerusalem" (2 Kings 24:8). The text in 2 Chronicles 36:9 reads, " Jehoiachin *was* eight years old when he began to reign, and he reigned three months and ten days in Jerusalem: and he did *that which was* evil in the sight of the LORD."

I admit that there are two different ages in the texts, one stating 8 years and the other 18. This is not the first time that something of this nature is mentioned in the Bible. I will give some examples, but let us be mature and honest about these questions and our answers. We all know that if a child at 8 years old is king, he is under supervision. He is declared heir-apparent by his father or the leaders but he is not the one making the decisions because he is too young for that. So Jehoiachin was made heir-apparent by his father when he was 8, but at the age of 18 he began to operate by himself.

Adam Engesath says the following, "When Jehoiachin was eight years old his father made him co-regent, so that he could be trained in the responsibilities of leading a kingdom. Jehoiachin then became officially a king at the age of eighteen upon his father's death."[9] So again I say there is not a problem with the different ages of the same person; one must understand the context in which it is written.

Another example of someone reigning at 8 years old is found in 2 Chronicles 34:1; "Josiah *was* eight years old when he began to reign, and he reigned in Jerusalem one and thirty years." But verse three seems to indicate that it is when he turned sixteen that he really exercised authority. 2Chronicles 34:3 states, 'For in the eighth year of his reign, while he was yet a boy, he began to seek the God of David his father, and in the twelfth year he began to purge Judah and Jerusalem of the high places, the Asherim, and the carved and the metal images.'

How many children did Michal, David's wife have?

One text says that Michal had no children and the other said she had five; 2 Samuel 6:23 and 2 Samuel 21:8. Which is right?

2 Samuel 6:23 reads, "Therefore Michal the daughter of Saul had no child unto the day of her death." And 2 Samuel 21:8 says, "But the king took the two sons of Rizpah the daughter of Aiah, whom she bare unto Saul, Armoni and Mephibosheth; and the five sons of Michal the daughter of Saul, whom she brought up for Adriel the son of Barzillai the Meholathite."

Now the text in 2 Samuel 6:23 states without a doubt that Michal, Saul's daughter died without having children. God had punished her because of the way she spoke to her

---

[9] Adam Engesath, *How old is Jehoiachin?* May 11, 2006, accessed 2016, http://www.thywordistrue.com/contradictions/17-how-old-is-jehoiachin

husband David, when he brought back the Ark of God; David was dancing before the Lord and Michal was displeased with the way David behaved. But God was displeased with Michal because of how she behaved towards David and shut up her womb so she never bore any children.

However there is another way one could be said to have children without them being biological. They can be adopted. And that is what the text in 2 Samuel 21:8 is referring to. It says "the five sons of Michal the daughter of Saul whom she brought up for Adriel the son of Barzillai the Meholathite." We must take note of the words 'whom she brought up for Adriel.' 'Brought up for' is saying that they were not her biological sons but Adriel's sons. Now remember that Adriel was married to Michal's sister. 1 Samuel 18:19 says, "But it came to pass at the time when Merab Saul's daughter should have been given to David, that she was given unto Adriel the Meholathite to wife." So she most probably adopted her own sister's sons. And that in a very quick and simple way dispels any claim of falsehood in the scriptures.

Chapter 14

Humanism Versus Christianity

Many agree with the concept of right and wrong. But who determines what is right and what is wrong? I believe that this is where humanism comes against Christianity.

For the Christian, God is the one who dictates what is right and wrong and these things are found in the Holy Scripture. On the other hand for the humanist, either he or society determines what is right or wrong. He does not go according to what God or any other supreme being says. For instance, for humanists, if two consenting adults agree to have sex, there is nothing wrong with that, even though they may be married to other people. God calls this adultery, a sin and therefore it is not right. But the humanist would beg to differ.

So the Christian's conflict with the humanist is that humanism does not accept God's definition of sin. But if human beings or our culture is our standard for living, then we don't have any standard because all cultures have different standards and every man would practice what he believes is right and wrong in his own eyes. This kind of philosophy is promoted by the devil. Ironic, since they will say that they are not being influenced by any supreme being.

We mere humans cannot make moral standards for ourselves because we ourselves are mutable, fallible and unholy. We need a perfect being to give us right standards. As A. C. Sproul says, "With God there is a definite and absolute black and white."[1]

This fight may look like it is physical but it is not. The devil is influencing many people to fight against the Word of God, but they do it under different headings and through different organizations and systems. People want separation from God. They want freedom to rebel even against the God who created them. It is like the people in Noah's days; "Therefore they say unto God, Depart from us; for we desire not the knowledge of thy ways. What *is* the Almighty, that we should serve him? and what profit should we have, if we pray unto him? (Job 21:14-15)

This philosophy of Humanism has been around a long time. It is just resurfacing and it is very aggressive and bold. This godless philosophy says, as long as it brings pleasure and money and it is legal, do it. Governments reason, once it will improve the economy, then do it. There is very little concern about fundamental values and the moral health of the people and nation.

God's Word versus Man's Word

From the very beginning there have been attacks against the Word of God. The first one came from the devil himself. "Now the serpent was more subtil than any beast of the field which the LORD God had made. And he said unto the

---

[1] Sproul, *Following Christ*, 301

woman, Yea, hath God said, Ye shall not eat of every tree of the garden?" (Genesis 3:1). So the first attack in the world was an attack against the Word of God. The devil said 'has God said'. God has spoken and it is up to us to either believe what God says or what man says. Believe God, and let every man be a liar.

In Genesis chapter one, it is recorded ten times that God 'said', and whatsoever He said came to pass. God created everything by His word. We can count on the Word of God. Again, I think it is important to note that the first being that questioned the Bible was the devil. Even when we don't quite understand why God says don't do something, we should abstain from doing it because God knows best. God has never been wrong. So we can trust him. We don't have to experiment. Contrary to some beliefs, we don't have to personally experience something to know that it is wrong.

We know that crack-cocaine is wrong because we see its effect on the people who take it. There are many ways we can know a thing including by observation and through experience. The doctor knows that we are sick, not because he ate what we ate, but by the symptoms. The judge knows that we are guilty, not because he did what we did but by the evidence. You don't have to personally experience a thing to know that it is true. We have to accept that God knows what is right and wrong. Man does not have the kind of knowledge that God has.

Now in these end-times, everything that God says is being challenged by man. For many today it is not what God says about creation, but what the scientist says; not what God says about marriage but what the Supreme Court says; not what God says about hell, but what the theologian says. Today it is man's word versus God's word. Man is claiming to be more brilliant than God. But, no matter how much man attacks the Holy Scriptures it will remain true. A preacher once said, "Tell me which book in the world has accurately described the times that we live in as the Bible?" The obvious answer is none.

God said to Noah, "I will destroy the world" and He did. The only people who were saved were those who obeyed God. Matthew 4:4 states, "But he answered and said, It is written, man shall not live by bread alone but by every word that proceedeth out of the mouth of God." Again, Jesus says in Matthew 24:35, "Heaven and earth shall pass away, but my words shall not pass away."

Mal Couch wrote, "Abraham Lincoln called the Bible 'the best gift God has given to man.'"[2] This is a very true statement. My prayer is that we would obey what the Bible says and not what man says against the Word of God.

Spirit versus Flesh

On this matter, the scripture says in Romans 8:8-9, "So then they that are in the flesh cannot please God. But ye are not in the flesh, but in the Spirit, if so be that the Spirit of God dwell in you. Now if any man have not the Spirit of Christ, he is none of his." Also, Galatians 5:17 reads, "For the flesh lusteth against the Spirit, and the Spirit against the flesh: and these are contrary the one to the other: so that ye cannot do the things that ye would."

When a person is born again, his spirit comes into relationship with God's Spirit and so there comes a conflict between pleasing God and pleasing self, or what is referred to as 'flesh'. Here the word 'flesh' stands for the carnal human

---

[2] Mal Couch, *Inspiration and Inerrancy: God Has Spoken*, (Chattanooga, TN: AMG Publishers, 2003), 5

nature which cannot please God. There are things in us that are not of God which we must destroy because they want to rule us; things like pride, evil thoughts, unforgiveness. Jesus says this on the matter: "That which is born of the flesh is flesh; and that which is born of the Spirit is spirit" (John 3:6).

So a man that is born only in the flesh cannot please God, because he is flesh. God is Spirit. And there is a principle; flesh and spirit cannot agree. We must be led either by flesh or by the spirit. And if we are led by flesh, we are not pleasing God. That is why we need to be born again; we need the Holy Spirit and the nature of God in us. And that is what happens when one is saved; he receives the divine nature in him, born of the Spirit.

The problem is that we have both the flesh and the spirit co-existing in us after salvation. So there is a war inside of us for domination. But we have the power of 'will' to select which of these we would allow to lead us. The choice is ours to make. And this is the struggle on earth; will we yield to what the Spirit of God says or what our sinful desires want us to do.

Sin versus Righteousness

There are people who are servants to sin and there are those who are servants of righteousness. It all depends on who their master is. Their actions and life-styles tell us who their master is. Romans 6:20 says, "For when ye were the servants of sin, ye were free from righteousness." Man's problem is a sin problem. Christ died because of man's sins, that He might set man free from sin. The greatest problem in the world is a sin problem. Because of sin, Adam went out of the garden and hid himself. Because of sin, Cain went out from the presence of God. The world is in the mess that it is today because of sin. Yet man continues to live sinful lives. By their own power, they are servants of sin. The only way to get out of sin is by allowing Jesus Christ to set you free from sin.

When Christ sets someone free, that person must become a servant of righteousness and not be entangled again with the yoke of bondage. A servant of righteousness cannot serve two masters. When he was serving sin, he did not care about righteousness. Once he turns to God he must not practice sin. It is by their fruits you shall know them; not just by their talk, but by their lifestyles.

There is a story in the Bible in the book of Numbers chapters 22 to 24, where Balak sent for Balaam to curse the children of Israel and despite all he did, he could not curse them because they were living uprightly. But in chapter 25 they fell into sin and twenty four thousand of them died because of their sin. When nothing else can destroy you, sin will, and there are many such examples in the Bible.

Another example is recorded in Joshua chapter 7 about Achan, and how Israel was defeated because of this man's sin. The Bible gives example after example of such occurrences. Yet there are many who choose to live a double life and some even teach that it is ok to live that way. Those who are saved by God's grace, do not continue living in sin; otherwise it is not grace, but disgrace.

The Principles of God versus The Principles of The Devil

The enemy tries his best to see that we follow his principles instead of God's. But we must guard our minds against the thoughts of the devil. In his book, Soul Detox, Craig Groeschel says, "Any thought that is not from God should be demolished, destroyed and annihilated. Instead of being prisoners of war, we take untrue thoughts captive and make them obedient to God's truth."[3]

We need to know what thoughts we can allow to take root in our minds because thoughts can lead to actions. Groeschel continues, "Weed the garden of your mind on a regular basis. What needs pruning? What needs to be nipped in the bud before it overtakes the fruit of the Spirit your soul longs to produce?"[4] The devil loves to plant evil thoughts in our minds. He cannot force us to obey him, but he can tempt us to do so. We must search our hearts and minds daily to ensure that our thoughts and actions are based on God's principles.

The Name of Jesus versus All Other Names

Isn't it surprising that in many places and nations laws have been passed that prohibit the mention of the name of Jesus? But why? In these same places one can mention the name of Allah, Mohammed, Krishna, Buddha or even God, but not the name of Jesus. Why? You see, the Bible says plainly that the only power that is above all the power of the enemy is the name of Jesus.

So the messengers of the devil, both human and demons, will fight hard so that the name of Jesus would be banned any and everywhere. The following scriptures tell us about the power that there is in the name of Jesus; "That at the name of Jesus every knee should bow, of *things* in heaven, and *things* in earth, and *things* under the earth;" (Philippians 2:10). "Neither is there salvation in any other: for there is

---

[3] Groeschel, *Soul Detox,* 41

[4] Ibid, 43

none other name under heaven given among men, whereby we must be saved." (Acts 4:12)

So, if that name is not mentioned people would not be saved, because salvation is only in His name. Satan would have a field day. The intention of the devil is to stop the name of Jesus from being mentioned so that people will forget there is a Jesus who can set them free from Satan and the sting of death.

The name is so important that even in our prayer to God we must pray in the name of Jesus, because the Word of God says, "And in that day ye shall ask me nothing. Verily, verily, I say unto you, Whatsoever ye shall ask the Father in my name, he will give *it* you" (John 16:23). But not only should we pray in the name of Jesus, but we can also cast out devils in the name of Jesus. So you understand why the devil loves to stop that name from being spoken. "And these signs shall follow them that believe; In my name shall they cast out devils; they shall speak with new tongues;" (Mark 16:17).

The name of a person is very important because there is meaning, value and intent in a name. If you are given the authority by the President to go to his home and tell his wife that he sent you and that she should give you one hundred dollars, once she is sure he is the one who sent you, then you won't have a problem.

"A person's name is more than just an identification of who they are. It carries with it the embodiment of their character standing, reputation and authority."[5] So at the proper use of the name of Jesus all authority bows.

Jesus has given us the right to use His name. If His name still has power it means that He is alive. His name means Savior, for the Word says He shall be called Jesus,

---

[5] Andy Pruitt, *The Power and Promises of the Name Jesus;* (Lulu-Borders, 2009), 21

'for he shall save his people from their sins" (Matthew 1:21). Kenneth E. Hagin said that "Kenyon Points out that men obtain great names in three ways. Some are born to a great name - a king, for instance. Others make their name great by their achievements. Still others have a great name conferred upon them. The more excellent Name came by all three means. Jesus' Name is great because He inherited a great Name. His Name is great because of His achievements. His Name is great because it was conferred upon Him."[6] It was conferred upon Him by God Almighty, not man.

The name of Jesus has all authority. It is known in Heaven. Angels bow to Him and obey His commands. It is known in earth. He came and died to save man. He is known under the earth; for sometime during His death and resurrection he went down to hell and set the captives free. "Now that he ascended, what is it but that he also descended first into the lower parts of the earth? He that descended is the same also that ascended up far above all heavens, that he might fill all things" (Ephesians 4:9-10).

> For Christ also hath once suffered for sins, the just for the unjust, that he might bring us to God, being put to death in the flesh, but quickened by the Spirit: By which also he went and preached unto the spirits in prison; Which sometime were disobedient, when once the longsuffering of God waited in the days of Noah, while the ark was a preparing, wherein few, that is, eight souls were saved by water (1 Peter 3:18-20).

---

[6] Kenneth E. Hagin, *The Name of Jesus;* (Tulsa, OK: Faith Library Publications, 1979), 13

So the name of Jesus is known everywhere in scriptures as being one with all power.

Creation versus Evolution

Ken Ham says, "We need to understand the times we live in and that the fundamental battle is God's Word versus man's word."[7] Man has taken a stand against God. They may not say it boldly but in their speech and action it is very clear. Ken says, "Genesis is the only book that provides an account of the origin of all the basic entities of life and the universe: the origin of life, of man, of government, of marriage, of culture, of nations, of death, of the chosen people, of sin, of diet and clothes, of the solar system....the list is almost endless."[8]

The Bible is very accurate, not just in relating what happened in the past, but also in its prediction of the future as it is unfolding in our day. The violence, the financial system, the social problems, the political systems, the environmental problems, sickness and diseases and we can go on and on. The Bible alone is spot-on and up-to-date on these matters. What it says is what we are seeing, yet men are rejecting it for human philosophy and saying that these things cannot be verified or properly explained. But the Bible has prophesied many things which have come to pass. And I guarantee you, that which is prophesied and is yet to be fulfilled will happen as the Bible has said. Not even the evolutionist can disprove the Bible's accuracy in predictive matters.

Belief matters. Your belief will shape your character and actions. The reason that so many persons now

---

[7] Ken Ham, *The Lie,* (Green Forest, AR: Master Books, 2012), 42

[8] Ham, *The Lie,* 82-83

practice suicide bombing is because of their belief. They believe that if they do these things for Allah they will be blessed in the other life. They think they have become a martyr for Allah, even though they have killed innocent persons. No matter how wrong their belief is, it shapes their character and practice. That is why we must know the truth.

Men of old shut the mouths of lions. True believers in God were not afraid to speak; they were not afraid to be thrown in the fire or beheaded. But now instead of shutting the mouths of the lions of evolution we are shutting our own mouths. We need men and women who will stand for the truth against the lies of evolution. The evolutionists keep shifting their theory but the truth does not change, even when it is rejected.

Truth remains truth even when we don't accept it. Truth does not become truth because it is accepted by us or by culture. God's truth has been rejected by cultures, individuals, or even nations, but that does not mean it was not the truth. For instance, Jesus was rejected by individuals and nations, though He was the truth and He spoke the truth. Yet they rejected Him.

Ken Ham stated from the very table of contents of his book, *The Lie*, "The reason people do not want to accept creation is that it means there is a Creator who sets the rules Thus, no person can write his own rules."[9] But man wants to do his own thing and he is trying to appease his conscience by saying it is ok. They say to themselves, 'let us say there is no God, therefore there will be no judgment." But this is self deception.

---

[9] Ham, *The Lie,* Table of Contents

It Is Not Flesh and Blood

There is a war going on. It is the greatest war ever, but it is not of flesh and blood. As the Bible says in Ephesians 6:12; "For we wrestle not against flesh and blood, but against principalities, against powers, against the rulers of the darkness of this world, against spiritual wickedness in high *places*."

So that fight is greater than any physical fight. For demons have more power than man. Therefore we need divine help to fight these demonic spirits. Thank God, through Jesus Christ humans can win this fight. So we can say we are not alone in this world. There is a physical and a spiritual, a world of flesh and blood and a world of spirit beings, good and evil.

"The existence of Satan cannot be determined by the opinions of men. The only source of information is the Bible. This is the reason why Satan tries to discredit the word of God."[10] We don't know about the spirit world because we are mere flesh and blood, but God has not left us ignorant.

The Bible says we are wrestling with spiritual powers. These principalities we are fighting against are well organized. Hammond said,

> The Greek word for principalities is archas. This word is used to describe things in a series such as leaders, rulers and magistrates. Thus a series of leaders or rulers would describe their rank and organization. So the word 'principalities' tells us that the satanic kingdom is highly organized. Perhaps Satan's

---

[10] Rev. Clarence Larkin, *The Spirit World*; (Philadelphia PA: Rev. Clarence Larkin Estate, 1921), 8

> forces are much the same in organization as
> the army of the United States which has the
> President as commander-in-chief, followed
> by generals, colonels, majors, captains,
> lieutenants on down to private.[11]

Maybe one thing which needs to be added to this quotation is that the army of Satan is much more organized than the United States Army, though the structure may be similar. Now although Satan has one third of the angels on his side, he still uses human beings to work for him against the Kingdom of God. Just as God has his people, Satan has his. But those who are with God are more than those who are with Satan; he only has one third of the angels.

It Is For Your Soul

The actual fight which exists is for our souls. Satan wants us to be suffering in hell with him but Jesus wants us to be with Him in Heaven forever. Jesus said, "For what shall it profit a man, if he shall gain the whole world, and lose his own soul? Or what shall a man give in exchange for his soul?" (Mark 8:36-37)

Jesus is saying there is nothing as valuable as your soul. Even though you have the whole world (which is improbable) but lose your soul, it will profit you nothing. So your soul is more profitable than the world. But, how can you lose your soul? If it is not in God's hands it is lost. If Satan is steering it, it is lost. If Christ is not the one controlling your soul, it is lost.

---

[11] Frank and Ida Mae Hammond, *Pigs in the Parlour: A Practical Guide to Deliverance;* (Impact Books, Inc. 1973), 14

"The soul can be fooled, betrayed, injured, abandoned, and tortured beyond endurance, but it cannot be killed."[12] This means it cannot be destroyed here on earth nor can it cease to exist. However, it has the capacity to feel pain and suffering as well as joy. So when talking about losing your soul, we are talking about your soul going to the place of torment; and in that sense we are referring to the real person.

Joseph A. Beet talking about the immortality of the soul said concerning Plato, "If the soul is really immortal, what care should be taken of her, not only in respect of the portion of time which is called life but of eternity and the danger of neglecting her from this point of view does indeed appear to be awful."[13] Man must prepare for his soul now. Never let it be lost because it will suffer in eternity if it is lost.

Beet continued, "Josephus (wars bk.11.8.11) reports that the Pharisees believed that the bodies are indeed corruptible but that the soul continue immortal always."[14] Nothing can eliminate the soul. It is our most precious possession. It cannot be extinguished even in the fire of hell, although it will be feeling the fire.

---

[12] Heyward Bruce Ewart, *Soul Rape, Recovering Personhood After Abuse,* (Place of publication not identified: Loving Healing Press, 2012), 127

[13] Joseph Agar Beet, *A Manual of Theology;* (London: Hodder and Stoughton, 1906), 518

[14] Beet, *A Manual of Theology,* 518

Chapter 15

Modern Battleground Issues

In this chapter we will examine the hot issues of abortion, capital punishment, homosexuality and child discipline.

Taking a stand on Abortion

Let's start with some scriptures on the matter; "Cursed *be* he that taketh reward to slay an innocent person. And all the people shall say, Amen" (Deuteronomy 27:25). In application of this text I will put the doctors who perform the abortions as those who take rewards to slay innocent blood. No one can be as innocent as a child in the womb. That child has not done anything to anyone, yet is killed.

God's Word asks for the protection of the unborn. Here is what it says in Exodus 21:22-23; "If men strive, and hurt a woman with child, so that her fruit depart *from her,* and yet no mischief follow: he shall be surely punished, according as the woman's husband will lay upon him; and he shall pay as the judges *determine.* And if *any* mischief follow, then thou shalt give life for life," (Exodus 21:22-23). The unborn child is protected by the law of God. If he loses his life, the one who caused the child to die must be put to death as well.

The book of Acts 17:28 says, "For in him we live, and move, and have our being; as certain also of your own poets have said, For we are also his offspring." We cannot kill God's offspring, especially those yet not born nor having committed any offense worthy of death.

God called us from our mothers' wombs. Galatians 1:15 reads, "But when it pleased God, who separated me from my mother's womb, and called *me* by his grace". So it is not man who has the power to cause conception; it is a work of God. Many people want children but cannot have. There are some who don't want any and use contraceptives, yet get pregnant. It is not at all in our power. Life comes from God. The innocent unborn child comes from God and He has a plan for that child. We must be careful not to destroy that plan.

Some of the church fathers opposed abortion very strongly. Caesarius of Arles wrote,

> No woman should take any drug to procure an abortion, because she will be placed before the judgment seat of Christ, whether she killed an already born child or a conceived one. Clement of Alexandria, in the second century AD, was even stronger in his choice of words: 'For those women who concealed sexual wantonness by taking stimulating drugs to bring on an abortion wholly lose their humanity along with the fetus.[1]

---

[1] Tom J. Obengo, *The Quest for Human Dignity in the Ethics of Pregnancy Termination*, (Eugene, OR: Wipf & Stock, 2016), 24

When Athenagoras, a Greek apologist for Christianity, was called upon to address the Emperor Marcus Aurelius in A.D. 177, he sought to answer the charge of cannibalism which stemmed from the Romans misunderstanding of the Eucharist. He stated that Christians could not even look at a murder much less participate in one.

We can go on and on about the church fathers who stood up against abortion, but that is not necessary; for indeed abortion was greatly rejected in this world. In many nations there were laws even to imprison people who practiced abortion. My nation was one of them. An abortion could only take place in case of rape, and if the mother's life was threatened. But now we don't want to obey what God says. We want to have our choice, even when that choice is to kill an innocent child. We say to God 'depart from us, we want none of your counsel.' One day He will say to those of us who live that way, 'depart from me, I never knew you.'

Wallbuilders.com, Foundation of Freedom Episode 7: The Bible and Science, carries an interesting article on abortion. "In a 1992 study, Arizona State University researcher Nancy Felipe Russo, PhD, analyzed the study population and concluded that most women suffer no long-term mental health repercussions when they abort an unintended first pregnancy. A decade later, David C. Reardon, PhD, looked at the data in a different way and concluded that abortion is linked to later depression."[2]

The preceding quotation was used to show that it depends on what side of the fence you are on. Unfortunately

---

[2] "Abortion and Depression: Is There a Link?" WebMD. October 31, 2005. Accessed January 31, 2017. http://www.webmd.com/depression/news/20051029/abortion-depression-is-there-link#1

some people, even medical personnel, have their own biases, but God is always right and knows best. If He says don't do it, He means don't do it and He knows why.

The website gave some reasons that women choose abortion. Here is what they say,

> Birth control (contraceptive) failure. Over half of the women who have an abortion used a contraceptive method during the month they became pregnant. Inability to support or care for a child. To end an unwanted pregnancy. To prevent the birth of a child with birth defects or severe medical problems. Such defects are often unknown until routine second-trimester tests are done. Pregnancy resulting from rape or incest. Physical or mental conditions that endanger then woman's health if the pregnancy is continued.[3]

They went on to say, "In the United States 9 out of 10 abortions are performed in the first 12 weeks (first trimester) of pregnancy. Most of these are done within the first 9 weeks of pregnancy."[4] You see many persons say that laws must be passed for abortion because of rape or medical conditions. The facts prove otherwise. People just want to go against the word of God and do their own thing.

Now it is not just the woman who is guilty here. Some men are guiltier about abortion than the women. At times they are

---

[3] Paul B. Fowler, *Abortion: Toward an Evangelical Consensus,* (Portland, OR: Multnomah Press, 1987), 17-18

[4] Fowler, *Abortion: Toward an Evangelical Consensus*

the ones who advise the women to have the abortion. Many times they provide the money for the murder and the support afterwards. Some of the men would go to the clinic with the women. One day God will judge the secret of man's heart.

There are many people who would like to adopt a child. There are also many places where persons can go for counseling if pregnant and having thoughts of killing the child. There are those who would love to save this precious gift. But most people go to the place that they know is a slaughter house for babies.

Taking a Stand on Capital Punishment

This subject is controversial even in church. There are a great number of people on either side of the argument. In the Old Testament there were a lot of offences that carried the death penalty as punishment. Some of those are not even regarded as an offense in some nations any more. Maybe the one the modern world is more concerned about is murder. In Genesis 9:6, the Word of God says the following: "Whoso sheddeth man's blood, by man shall his blood be shed: for in the image of God made he man."

The other one we may still be very concerned about today is rape. Deuteronomy 22:25 says, "But if a man find a betrothed damsel in the field, and the man force her, and lie with her: then the man only that lay with her shall die." But it also applied to sins like fornication, as we read in Deuteronomy 22:13-21;

> If any man take a wife, and go in unto her, and hate her, And give occasions of speech against her, and bring up an evil name upon her, and say, I took this woman, and

when I came to her, I found her not a maid:
Then shall the father of the damsel, and
her mother, take and bring forth *the tokens
of* the damsel's virginity unto the elders of
the city in the gate: And the damsel's father
shall say unto the elders, I gave my daughter
unto this man to wife, and he hateth her;
And, lo, he hath given occasions of speech
against her, saying, I found not thy daughter
a maid; and yet these *are the tokens of* my
daughter's virginity. And they shall spread
the cloth before the elders of the city. And
the elders of that city shall take that man
and chastise him; And they shall amerce
him in an hundred *shekels* of silver, and
give *them* unto the father of the damsel,
because he hath brought up an evil name
upon a virgin of Israel: and she shall be his
wife; he may not put her away all his days.
But if this thing be true, *and the tokens of*
virginity be not found for the damsel: Then
they shall bring out the damsel to the door
of her father's house, and the men of her
city shall stone her with stones that she die:
because she hath wrought folly in Israel, to
play the whore in her father's house: so shalt
thou put evil away from among you.

Leviticus 20:10 speaks of adultery; "And the man that
committeth adultery with *another* man's wife, *even he* that
committeth adultery with his neighbour's wife, the adulterer
and the adulteress shall surely be put to death." These all
were punishable by death.

Now what do we say on these things? There had been some changes from the law of the Old Testament to the New Testament. Fornication was no longer punishable by death and neither was adultery. But both remained a great sin; though not punishable by death. John 8:3-11 reads,

> And the scribes and Pharisees brought unto him a woman taken in adultery; and when they had set her in the midst, They say unto him, Master, this woman was taken in adultery, in the very act. Now Moses in the law commanded us, that such should be stoned: but what sayest thou? This they said, tempting him, that they might have to accuse him. But Jesus stooped down, and with *his* finger wrote on the ground, *as though he heard them not.* So when they continued asking him, he lifted up himself, and said unto them, He that is without sin among you, let him first cast a stone at her. And again he stooped down, and wrote on the ground. And they which heard *it,* being convicted by *their own* conscience, went out one by one, beginning at the eldest, *even* unto the last: and Jesus was left alone, and the woman standing in the midst. When Jesus had lifted up himself, and saw none but the woman, he said unto her, Woman, where are those thine accusers? hath no man condemned thee? She said, No man, Lord. And Jesus said unto her, Neither do I condemn thee: go, and sin no more.

Here Jesus told the woman not to do it again; but he did not order to have her stoned. We have another example of something similar in the epistle of 1 Corinthians 5:1-5;

> It is reported commonly *that there is* fornication among you, and such fornication as is not so much as named among the Gentiles, that one should have his father's wife. And ye are puffed up, and have not rather mourned, that he that hath done this deed might be taken away from among you. For I verily, as absent in body, but present in spirit, have judged already, as though I were present, *concerning* him that hath so done this deed, In the name of our Lord Jesus Christ, when ye are gathered together, and my spirit, with the power of our Lord Jesus Christ, To deliver such an one unto Satan for the destruction of the flesh, that the spirit may be saved in the day of the Lord Jesus.

In the above text, Paul did not recommend the death penalty, neither could he, because it was not part of that nation's laws. So Paul recommended that the one who had committed such sins should be excommunicated from the church, and if he changed, then he should be re-accepted.

Homosexuality was to be punished by death. Leviticus 20:13 says, "If a man also lie with mankind, as he lieth with a woman, both of them have committed an abomination: they shall surely be put to death; their blood *shall be* upon them." But now in many nations homosexuals could even be legally 'married'.

Some of these examples were drawn from scripture to show that when we talk about capital punishment we must not just say 'well the scripture says they must be killed". But we need to examine to which offences the death penalty should be applied today. Is it just for murder or all the others the Bible speaks of? When listed there is a total of 18 different sins in the Old Testament that are punishable by death. Most of these are not reiterated in the New Covenant as worthy of death, but a case can be made for intentional murder.

Brett Kunkle in a blog on the Stand to Reason website (str.org) in a piece entitled, 'Is there Biblical Justification for Capital Punishment' states,

"When we turn to the pages of the New Testament, we do not find much data regarding the death penalty. However, it does seem that capital punishment was assumed in the New Testament. First, we find that governing authorities may practice capital punishment. Romans 13:3–4 states that "rulers are not a cause of fear for good behavior, but for evil…. [I]f you do what is evil, be afraid; for it does not bear the sword for nothing; for it is a minister of God, an avenger who brings wrath upon the one who practices evil." Furthermore, in Acts 25:11, the Apostle Paul addresses Festus and the tribunal: "If then I am a wrongdoer, and have committed anything worthy of death, I do not refuse to die; but if none of those things is true of which these men accuse me, no one can hand me over to them. I appeal to Caesar." In these passages, it seems that the State is justified in using the death penalty to keep order."[5]

---

[5] Brett Kunkle, "Is There Biblical Justification for Capital Punishment," Stand To Reason (web log), February 22, 2017. Accessed October 10, 2017, www.str.org.

The tenor of the New Covenant shows that we must try our best to restore people, even after they have committed a grave sin. Maybe we have not focused our time and energy on restoring people enough. People can and do change, but will we make the sacrifice to help them? Now this is not to say that there may not be instances where capital punishment will have to be administered for the safety of others and the nation, but our first response should be to help restore the person. Capital punishment should be our last resort.

Taking a Stand on Child Discipline

Raising a child in this world is very hard. Therefore we must be well equipped to do so. To have virtuous children discipline becomes one of the necessities. When we talk about discipline we are not talking about punishment, although there may be an aspect of punishment or sacrifice in discipline. "Discipline means shaping behavior and modifying personal tendencies so that eventually children are guided by inner rules."[6] They should be guided by inner rules, not just by the fear of punishment.

We have been given the responsibility to raise children and one day we will have to stand before God and give an account for them. A lot of people don't discipline their children and on the other hand many who think they are disciplining are simply abusing them. "Discipline allows short-term pain for long-term pleasure; permissiveness

---

[6] William and Martha Sears, *The Complete Book of Christian Parenting and Child Care: a Medical and Moral Guide to Raising Happy Healthy Children,* (Nashville: B&H Pub. Group, 1997), 25

allows short-term pleasure for long-term pain."[7] What the child may want now might not be what is right for him at the moment and parents must make their children understand that. But in order to make the child understand, you must have a loving relationship with that child. You must let the child know why it is not ok to have a thing right now. Sadly, some parents refuse to discipline their children; all that the children ask of them, they give.

We must teach our children about the Lord from a very young age. That was one of the mandates God gave in the Old Testament. Parents were to write the Word of God where their children could see it every day. They were to keep the yearly feast, that their children would know how God had delivered them and blessed them. If we want righteous children we must teach them about the Lord in words and in our actions. Proverbs 1:7a says, "The fear of the LORD *is* the beginning of knowledge..."

---

[7] Larry and Judi Keefauver, *77 Irrefutable Truths of Parenting,* (Bridge-Logos Foundation, 2001), 37

Bibliography

"Animal Welfare: Germany Moves to Ban Bestiality." *BBC News.* November 28, 2012. http://www.bbc.com (accessed 2016).

Beach, Waldo. *Christain Ethics in the Protestant Tradition.* Atlanta, GA: John Knox Press, 1988.

Beet, Joseph Agar. *A Manual of Theology.* London: Hodder and Stoughton, 1906.

Blanco, Juan Ignacio. "David Koresh." *Murderpedia.* www.murderpedia.org (accessed 2016).

Boyles, Salynn. *Abortion and Depression: Is There a Link?* October 31, 2005. www.webmd.com (accessed January 31, 2017).

Bromiley, Geoffrey W., Gerhard Kittel, and Gerhard Friedrich. *Theological Dictionary of the New Testament.* Grand Rapids, MI: Eerdmans, 2006.

Bullinger, E. W. *The Companion Bible Condensed; Commentary on Exodus 12:40.* Kregel Publication, 1995.

Carpenter, Eugene E. *Holman Treasury of Key Bible Words; 200 Greek and 200 Hebrew Words Defined and Explained.* Nashville, TN: Holman Reference, 2000.

Charles, Colson, and Anne Morse. *Burden of Truth.* Wheaton, IL: Tyndale House, 1997.

Clarke, Adam. *Adam Clarke's Commentary Practical and Explanatory on the Whole Bible.* Grand Rapids, MI: Baker Book House, 1967.

Couch, Mal. *Inspiration and Inerrancy: God Has Spoken.* Chattanooga, TN: AMG Publishers, 2003.

Engesath, Adam. "How Old is Jeoiachin." *Thy Word Is true.* May 11, 2006. http://www.thywordistrue.com (accessed 2016).

Enns, Paul P. *The Moody Handbook of Theology.* Chicago, IL: Moody Press, 2014.

Ewart, Heyward Bruce. *Soul Rape, Recovering Personhood After Abuse.* Loving Healing Press, 2012.

Fausset, A. R., David Brown, and Robert Jamieson. *Jamieson, Fausset & Brown's Commentary on the Whole Bible.* Grand Rapids, MI: Zondervan, 1961.

Fowler, Paul B. *Abortion: Toward an Evangelical Consensus.* Portland, OR: Multnomah Press, 1987.

Gabriel, Mark A. *Islam and Terrorism.* Lake Mary, Florida: Charisma House, 2002.

Geisler, Norman L. *Christain Ethics: Contemporary Issues & Options.* Grand Rapids, MI: Baker Academic, 2010.

Grenz, Stanley J. *Theology for the Community of God.* Grand Rapids, MI: William B. Eerdmans Pub. Co., 1994.

Groeschel, Craig. *Soul Detox: Clean Living in a Contaminated World.* Grand Rapids, MI: Zondervan, 2012.

Groothuis, Douglas. *Christianity That Counts; Being a Christian in a Non-Christian World.* Grand Rapids, MI: Baker Books, 1994.

Hagin, Kenneth E. *The Name of Jesus.* Tulsa, OK: Faith Library Publications, 1979.

Halverson, Dean. *The Illustrated Guide to World Religions.* Bloomington: Bethany House Publishers, 2003.

Ham, Ken. *The Lie.* Green Forest, AR: Master Books, 2012.

Ham, Ken, Andrew Smelling, and Carl Wieland. *The Answers Book: Answers to the 12 Most Asked Questions on Genesis and Creation/Evolution.* Sunnybank, Australia: Creation Science Foundation Ltd., 1990.

Hammond, Frank and Ida Mae. *Pigs in the Parlour: A Practical Guide to Deliverance.* Impact Books, Inc., 1973.

Henry, Matthew. *An Axposition of the Old and New Testament.* London: Thoms Printer, 1839.

—. *An Exposition of the Old and New Testament.* New York: Robert Carter and Brothers, 1865.

Hiebert, Paul G., R. Daniel Shaw, and Tite Tienou. *Understanding Folk Religion.* Grand Rapids, MI: Baker Books, 1999.

Hill, David G., and Peter C. Benner. *Baker Encyclopedia of Psychology and Counseling.* Grand Rapids, MI: Baker Books, 1999.

"How to Use Reasoning From the Scriptures." *Watchtower Online Library.* www.wol.jw.org (accessed September 3, 2016).

Johnson, B. W. *The People's New Testament.* Nashville, TN: Gospel Advocate Co., 1891.

Keefauver, Larry and Judi. *Irrefutable Truths of Parenting.* Bridge-Logos Foundation, 2001.

Kennedy, D. James, and Jerry Newcombe. *What's Wrong With Same Sex Marriage.* Wheaton, IL: Crossway Books, 2004.

Kunkle, Brett. "Is There Biblical Justification for Capital Punishment." *Stand To Reason.* February 22, 2017. www.str.org (accessed October 10, 2017).

Larkin, Rev. Clarence. *The Spirit World.* Philadelphia, PA: Clarence Larkin Estate, 1921.

Livingstone, F. L. Cross and E. A. *The Oxford Dictionary of The Christian Church.* Oxford: Oxford University Press, 2009.

McDowell, Josh, and Bob Hostetler. *Beyond Belief to Convictions.* Wheaton, IL: Tyndale House Publishers, 2002.

McDowell, Josh, and John Stewart. *Handbook of Today's Religion.* Nashville, TN: Thomas Nelson Publishers, 1983.

Minirth, Frank. *The Minirth Guide for Christian Counselors.* Nashville, TN: B&H Publishing Group, 2003.

Morey, Robert A. *The New Atheism and the Erosion of Freedom.* Las Vegas, NV: Christian Scholars Press, 2000.

Obengo, Tom J. *The Quest for Human Dignity in the Ethics of Pregnancy Termination.* Eugene, OR: Wipf & Stock, 2016.

Oxford Learner's Dictionary: Pornography. January 19, 2015. http://www.oxfordlearnersdictionaries.com (accessed 2016).

Pruitt, Andy. *The Power and Promises of the Name of Jesus.* Lulu-Borders, 2009.

Robertson, A. T. *Word Pictures in the New Testament.* Nashville, TN: B&H Publishing Group, 2000.

Ryrie, Charles Caldwell. *Basic Theology: A Popular Systematic Guide to Understanding Biblical Truth.* Chicago, IL: Moody Press, 1999.

Sauer, Richard, and Linda Sauer. *Answers in Genesis.* March 29, 2007. http://www.answersingenesis.org (accessed May 26, 2017).

Schnoebelen, William. *Masonry: Beyond the Light.* Chino, CA: Chick Publications, 1991.

Sears, William and Mary. *The Complete Book of Christian Parenting and Child Care: a Medical and Moral Guide to Raising Happy Healthy Children.* Nashville, TN: B&H Publishing Group, 1997.

Sproul, R. C. *Following Christ.* Wheaton, IL: Tyndale House Publishers Inc, 1983.

Spurgeon, C. H. *The Cheque Book of the Bank of Faith.* New York: Armstrong and Son, 1889.

Stevens, Selwyn. *The New Age: The Old Lie in a New Package.* New Zealand: Jubilee Resources International Inc., 2002.

Stone, Howard W. *Creative Pastoral Counseling Series: Crisis Counseling.* Minneapolis, MN: Fortress Press, 2009.

"Suicide." *Meriam-WebsterIncorporated.* www.merriam-webster.com/dictionary/suicide (accessed August 9, 2017).

Tenny, Merrill C. *The Zondervan Pictorial Encyclopedia of the Bible.* Grand Rapids, MI: Regency Reference Library, 1989.

Thayer, J. H. "Thayer's Greek Definitions." March 16, 2012.

Thiessen, Henry Clarence. *Lectures in Systematic Theology.* Grand Rapids, MI: William B. Eerdmans Pub. Co., 1989.

Torrey, R. A., Canne, Browne, Blaney, Scott, and et al. *Treasury of Scripture Knowledge.* London: Samuel Bagster and Sons Ltd, 14th Edition.

Walvoord, John F.; Zuck, Ray B. *The Bible Knowledge Commentary on Matthew, An Exposition of the Scriptures by Dallas Seminary Faculty.* Victory Books, 1983.

Wright, H. Norman. *The Complete Guide to Crisis and Trauma Counseling; What to do and Say When It Matters Most.* Ventura, California: Regal/From Gospel Light, 2011.

About the Author

Bishop Thomas Eristhee was converted in his teens. He spent many years in the church learning about God and all aspects of ministry and then felt the Spirit of God impressing him to attend Bible School. After a few years of indecision, he heeded God's call upon his life.

Bishop Eristhee holds a diploma from the West Indies School of Theology, and received his Bachelor of Arts Degree from the Caribbean College of the Bible International. He has a Master of Ministry Degree with Trinity Theological Seminary, and obtained his DMin with Covington Seminary, and a PhD in Apologetics with Evangelical Theological Seminary.

Thomas Eristhee has written five other books namely, What To Do After Being Saved; The Church Revealed; Satan Exposed; What Should We Believe, Creation or Evolution; and Praying and Fasting, The Bible way

He is currently the Bishop for the Pentecostal Assemblies of the West Indies, (St. Lucia District). Bishop Eristhee has been married for 30 years to his wife, Midran. They have two children, Shimea and Jeremiah.

Printed in the United States
By Bookmasters